P9-DTW-782

once
a·day

Country

FAITH

ZONDERVAN

ZONDERVAN
Once-a-Day Country Faith
Copyright © 2013 by Zondervan

Requests for information should be addressed to:
Zondervan, Grand Rapids, Michigan 49530

Frames and background images: istockphoto
Cover and interior design: Jamie DeBruyn
Content provider: Deborah Evans Price

Printed in China

13 14 15 16 17 18 19 20 / GSC / 15 14 13 12 11 10 9 8 7 6 5 4 3 2 1

APRIL 2014

FOREWORD

When I was growing up in Hannah, SC, church was the first place I ever sang in front of a crowd. I was very fortunate to be brought up in a good Christian home where my parents encouraged me to chase my dreams and sometimes pushed me to when I was scared or insecure. It didn't take long for me to realize God had given me a special talent to sing and make music.

I moved to Nashville and had stars in my eyes and dreamt of all the money I was going to make and the fancy house I was going to live in. Then, through a fan, I was humbled. That fan shared with me how my song, "Long Black Train," had saved her life. It was then that I realized that I wasn't just doing this for me. I had a platform, and I could use it or abuse it. I started thinking about how my heroes like Randy Travis and John Anderson had inspired me and gotten me through tough times in my life via their music. Music is powerful if you allow it to be.

I don't consider myself the greatest singer or the greatest songwriter to ever exist, but I will tell you that I'm the best that I can be because I've given it 110% every time I've had the opportunity to set foot in a studio or on a stage. If I can help just a handful of people through my music, then what I've done has not been in vain. In this day and time, the Bible has been escorted out of our entertainment industries. It's not "cool" anymore to talk about Jesus or God or what the Bible has to say. This book you're about to read is proof that there are artists today that still believe in the power of music. They still believe in a loving God. They still believe that the words of the Bible are meaningful and relevant today. I'm honored to be in the company of this group of artists and to know that I'm not the only one trying to make a difference through the songs I sing. Sit back, turn off the TV, turn off the phone and enjoy this inspiring book. You'll be glad you did.

Josh Turner

WELCOME TO

Country FAITH

With so many stories that resonate with our souls and touch our hearts, there's a lot to love about country music. It's no wonder country music is the no.1 radio format among adults. Maybe you're one of the 95 million country music fans in the United States or one of the countless millions of fans from around the world. Wherever you are, you're holding an exclusive backstage pass to experience the faith of today's top country music stars as never before. With contributions from 56 of today's classic and rising country artists, *Once-A-Day Country Faith* includes the Bible passage that tops each of their charts as well as the reasons why this passage of Scripture is so valuable to them.

The editors at Zondervan are indebted to Deborah Evans Price, a veteran writer who has covered country, gospel and rock music for *Billboard* magazine since 1994, for her efforts to track down and interview so many artists. From grabbing a quick conversation backstage at the Grand Ole Opry in Nashville to chatting while riding around town in a pickup truck, Deborah asked each artist one simple question: "What passage from the Bible is the most meaningful to you—and why?" And now you're holding the answer.

Zondervan is also pleased to present a portion of the sale of every book to Sophia's Heart Foundation in Nashville, Tennessee, founded by *American Idol* finalist and country artist Danny Gokey.

After reading *Country Faith,* you too will be inspired to identify the Bible passage that means the most to you. And you'll listen to your favorite country artists in a whole new way. Kick back and settle in for an intimate journey into the heart, soul and faith of country music while discovering fresh insights into the One who promises to put a new song in our hearts (see Psalm 40:3).

TABLE OF CONTENTS

RANDY Owen

Again, truly I tell you that if two of you on earth agree about anything they ask for, it will be done for them by my Father in heaven. For where two or three gather in my name, there am I with them.
MATTHEW 18:19–20

Whether you're on the battlefield with hundreds of others, or there's just two or three of you on the road traveling, wherever you are, you can say a prayer and know you're being heard because that's what Scripture says. It's comforting to me. My daddy always quoted Matthew 18:19–20 so naturally. It's meant a lot to me over the years and still does.

I believe in the power of prayer, especially when two or more are gathered in his name. Every year country artists, along with record company and radio folks gather at St. Jude Children's Research Hospital in Memphis for a seminar to work on Country Cares for St. Jude Kids®. There are also fundraisers held throughout the year by country radio stations. When I look at the number of children who are alive today because of Country Cares, I think that's the greatest accomplishment of country radio. This year before I went to Memphis, I visited my mother and told her, "I want you to pray for me and pray with me because it's such an important weekend." It's always comforting to me to know we can gather together to pray and God hears us.

7

Jesus stopped and called them. "What do you want me to do for you?" he asked. "Lord," they answered, "we want our sight." Jesus had compassion on them and touched their eyes. Immediately they received their sight and followed him. **MATTHEW 20:32–34**

I have many favorite Bible passages. This one is about praying bold prayers. Jesus knew the men were blind. It took bold faith to believe their sight could be restored. They didn't ask for simple happiness, they asked for a miracle—something bold. It reminds me to ask him to help me see his plan during the dark times. Don't ask to just pass the class with a C grade. Ask for an A. God responds to big, bold prayers in a big, bold way. Ask for the faith, the vision, the guidance. Pray beyond your dreams. Pray for God to take it to the supernatural. I believe we should pray for others this way. God doesn't ask for our prayers to be logical and practical. He says just have faith.

PHOTO: JEREMY COWART

For I am convinced that neither death nor life, neither angels nor demons, neither the present nor the future, nor any powers, neither height nor depth, nor anything else in all creation, will be able to separate us from the love of God that is in Christ Jesus our Lord. ROMANS 8:38–39

This Scripture says that you are always loved no matter what. I love all the commas in these verses—neither death, nor life, nor angels, nor demons. It's so powerful. Nothing in the world can separate us and that's so comforting. The thing that draws me to it as an adult is the way it reminds us of God's unconditional love. I love it because it basically says, "You can make a mistake and it's okay." There's nothing that can separate us from God's love. Just knowing that in my heart brings comfort. When I've messed up or when I need to know that I'm loved no matter what, I can think of that Scripture and feel peace.

They are important verses for everyone to hear. I feel like there are probably so many people out there that stay away from God and from God's love because they think: "I'm not good enough." To me, that's the devil talking and getting in your head saying, "You're not good enough. Look at all these things that you do. There's too many things in your past and in your present, too many things in the world that make you not good enough for God's love." That's just NOT true because this Scripture tells us absolutely nothing can separate us. Look at all of the examples that it uses—neither the present, nor future, nor powers, nor height nor depth. It just doesn't matter. It's just knowing that your creator loves you unconditionally.

CARRIE
Underwood

BELLAMY
Brothers

HOWARD BELLAMY

What good is it for someone to gain the whole world, yet forfeit their soul? Or what can anyone give in exchange for their soul? MARK 8:36–37

These have always stood out as very potent words from Jesus. I think they are even more meaningful today in the society and culture we live in. Verse 36 explains the value of the soul and poses the question: "What good will it do for a person to gain the whole world but lose their soul?" This puts a lot of things in perspective in a world that more than ever borders on being totally material, transparent and phony. Verse 37 goes on to ask the question: "What will a man give in exchange for his own soul?" This question is timeless and, depending on how you believe and how you were raised, could be answered many ways. Speaking for myself, I value my soul over possessions even though I am as guilty as anyone of coveting a new truck or some other material thing. I think that's human nature. We just have to reel ourselves back in and read Jesus' words from Mark 8.

DAVID BELLAMY

If any of you lacks wisdom, you should ask God, who gives generously to all without finding fault, and it will be given to you. But when you ask, you must believe and not doubt, because the one who doubts is like a wave of the sea, blown and tossed by the wind. That person should not expect to receive anything from the Lord. Such a person is double-minded and unstable in all they do. JAMES 1:5–8

This is a favorite passage of mine because it explains asking God to answer your prayers in such a direct way. It also explains how important complete faith is and how God will not tolerate sitting on the fence. As a famous former fence sitter myself, I understand what it's like to go from asking for God's help without committing to staying faithful to trying to stay faithful when asking for God's favor. Like myself, I think most people read the first verse about praying for what they want while trying to overlook the verse about not wavering. But verse six is really the key to the three verses. And then if you go into verse eight, which reads, "Such a person is double-minded and unstable in all they do," it's fairly plain to see that no prayers are going to be answered without the faith that God demands.

CANAAN Smith

That Scripture has been my saving grace a lot of times, and I actually have it on a plaque in my house. Just when I think I've got everything figured out, and I know what's next, things will take a turn. I just have to walk by faith and realize that God knows what he is doing—and whatever happens is for my best. That really keeps you sane because nothing is consistent except God's promises and love for us.

PHOTO: SARAH BARLOW.

15

PHOTO: KRISTIN BARLOWE

KRISTY LEE Cook

For God so loved the world that he gave his one and only Son, that whoever believes in him shall not perish but have eternal life. JOHN 3:16

One of the very first Bible passages I memorized was John 3:16. It was hanging on our bathroom wall and didn't need any explanation at all. This verse has always just made perfect sense to me. I've always thought, How can anyone argue that? How can anyone not believe when it says it right there? The Bible is never wrong and will never be wrong. It helps heal the broken, lifts spirits, comforts, encourages and reassures us of everything we need to know. It has helped me through my own trials and tribulations.

I can't sit here and say that I have a favorite or most meaningful verse from the Bible. There's a lot of hope, guidance and wisdom in God's Word. Every day there's a verse that applies to what I'm going through, so to me it's all meaningful. The one I'm going to single out though is one that Christians and non-Christians alike are familiar with. That verse is John 3:16. We've all seen this Scripture verse referenced in numerous ways, even at sporting events!

This verse captures so many things in a short number of words. It says that God loves us so much that he sacrificed the life of his only Son! Jesus paid the ultimate price for our wrongdoing. All we have to do to receive eternal life is believe in him. It may sound simple, but that's because it is! We don't have to go to church or give all of our money to the poor or work at a soup kitchen three times a week or pray at certain hours and say certain things to receive a life that's everlasting. Not that all those things are bad, but they're not what really counts. Once you believe in Jesus Christ and accept his will for your life, you will want to help the poor and needy. You will want to give your time and money. You will want to live a clean life. That's the beauty of it. If a child "believes" in his parents, he will strive to please them and make them proud. And he will be blessed for it. God loves each and every one of us and wants us to spend our lives hereafter with him.

PHOTO: GEORGE HOLZ

DUSTIN *Lynch*

In their hearts humans plan their course, but the LORD establishes their steps.
PROVERBS 16:9

Proverbs 16:9 is a verse that I truly believe in and live by. We can all schedule and plan our lives, but the "great plan" of our lives is in God's hands.

I was in a really frustrating stretch of my life and could not figure out if music was my calling. One night I hopped out of bed, walked down to the basement, grabbed a guitar and wrote a prayer titled "Your Plan" (the bonus track on my first album). I surrendered myself to God as I wrote the lyrics, "This is my white flag wave / This is me handing you the reigns / I know You can steer my hurricane." At that moment I let him take over and stopped worrying about my plans, the journey of my life. This whole crazy ride is in his hands. It's his plan.

ERIC *Paslay*

I can do all this through him who gives me strength.
PHILIPPIANS 4:13

Philippians 4:13 often comes to mind. If it's God's will in your life and you follow it, even if it involves things you don't think you are capable of, then he will open up doors. It's all in his perfect timing, and I'm not putting my happiness in just me singing songs on the radio. It makes me really happy to play and sing for people, but I'm glad I'm getting my songs recorded with other voices singing them. It actually means a lot to me that other people want to record songs I've written.

JANIE *Fricke*

I lift up my eyes to the mountains—
 where does my help come from?
My help comes from the LORD,
 the Maker of heaven and earth.

He will not let your foot slip—
 he who watches over you will not slumber;
indeed, he who watches over Israel
 will neither slumber nor sleep.

The LORD watches over you—
 the LORD is your shade at your right hand;
the sun will not harm you by day,
 nor the moon by night.

The LORD will keep you from all harm—
 he will watch over your life;
the LORD will watch over your coming
 and going
 both now and forevermore. PSALM 121

I've been a church go'er all my life. Over the past couple of years I've joined a weekly Bible study, and it's been a wonderful learning process. I've been inspired by some of the Scriptures that I've studied. We studied Psalm 121, went through it line by line and took it apart. I memorized it and decided to put music to it. One day I picked up my guitar and the melody came out and the chords came out. It's hard to write a song to a psalm that is not perfectly rhymed, so I wasn't sure how to get through it, but I did. I put a simple, pretty melody to it and played it for my husband. He thinks I should try to put music to several psalms and record them.

I've had a lot of friends who have been in sad, tragic situations lately, and Psalm 121 immediately comes to mind. I quote it to them: "I lift my eyes up to the mountains—where does my help come from? My help comes from the LORD, the Maker of heaven and earth" (Psalm 121:1). Those words are very comforting. When you say a prayer and ask the Lord to walk with you by your side when you're going into a tough situation, you can actually feel his presence. That feeling is amazing.

He will cover you with his feathers,
and under his wings you will find refuge;
his faithfulness will be your shield and rampart. PSALM 91:4

One of the passages of Scripture that has always meant the most to me is Psalm 91:4. I'm a guy who loves to make music, and I love to write songs. This is what I do and this is my life. Psalm 91 is basically my mantra. I wouldn't have written any songs if I didn't write about the truth. I wouldn't have anything to write. I have never written a song that I've just made up. Everything I've written has been something that has happened to me in a moment of inspiration colliding with desperation.

BILLY RAY *Cyrus*

I never had anything that was ever in the middle of the road. It was either really, really bad or really, really good. Nothing's ever in the middle. That's just the way my life has been, so I'm just putting down in the truth and that truthfulness I think echoes loudly through my music.

PHOTO: RUSS HARRINGTON

TRISHA *Yearwood*

Every good and perfect gift is from above, coming down from the Father of the heavenly lights, who does not change like shifting shadows. JAMES 1:17

When I made my first record for MCA in 1991, I wanted to thank God for all his blessings, but I didn't want to sound trite or insincere. I decided that rather than just saying thank you, I'd find a Bible verse and put it in the liner notes of the album. If folks wanted to look up the verse for themselves, that was good by me.

I picked James 1:17 for that record, because I believe with all my heart that everything good in my life comes from God. I truly believe he gave me the gift of music, and he expected me to use it.

Over the years, I've included a Bible verse in every studio album I've made. It's my way of expressing my faith. I don't wear it on my sleeve, but it's always there.

When I made that first album I was 26 years old. I didn't have the life experience I have now, over 20 years later. I hadn't lost my father and mother. I didn't know just how much I would need that faith. I don't think that I could face every day if I didn't believe that God existed; if I didn't believe that one day I would see my precious parents again.

This may sound simple, but I think our world could stop fighting over all of the differences in religion if we all realized that we really believe the same thing. God, by any name you choose, is love. It's that simple.

EASTON *Corbin*

I was raised in church, and my dad really knows the Bible. He's shared a lot of verses with me over the years, and John 14:12–15 is one that really struck a chord with me. It basically says that God makes a way for us. If we keep his commandments, whatever we ask of him, he'll give to us. As for me, he gave me the opportunity to make a living making music.

I've been singing since I was a kid. This is all I've ever wanted to do, and God's finally giving me the opportunity to do it. But like my Dad says, "To whom much is given, much is expected." Along with all the success that I've had, come many expectations. Because people see me out there every day, especially young people, I want to be as good of an example as I can be. It's all about following what God says. You can get out on this road and get lost pretty quickly if you aren't careful. You've got to keep his commandments.

PHOTO: JIM WRIGHT

LAUREN *Alaina*

"For I know the plans I have for you," declares the LORD, "plans to prosper you and not to harm you, plans to give you hope and a future." JEREMIAH 29:11

I absolutely LOVE this Bible verse. No matter what kind of obstacles life throws your way, God is always there and watching over you. It provides such a sense of comfort, even in the hardest times. Knowing he is watching over me makes all my fears disappear.

KIEFER *Thompson*

(THOMPSON SQUARE)

PHOTO: ANTHONY BAKER

But seek first his kingdom and his righteousness, and all these things will be given to you as well. MATTHEW 6:33

Matthew 6:33 has been a constant reminder to us as a band about what our priorities should be and how to make, through faith, our goals a reality. It gave us a peace during all the hard times and continues to do so as we take this musical journey together.

PHOTO COURTESY OF BILLY DEAN

Love is patient, love is kind. It does not envy, it does not boast, it is not proud. It does not dishonor others, it is not self-seeking, it is not easily angered, it keeps no record of wrongs. Love does not delight in evil but rejoices with the truth. It always protects, always trusts, always hopes, always perseveres. 1 CORINTHIANS 13:4–7

This Scripture verse is a cornerstone of my whole religious belief system, because it tells you what love is, and the Bible says that God is love. That's how I live my life. That's the thing that guides my parenting. I've got to obey that Scripture. If I can perfect that, if I can love, then I will be more God-like.

My favorite part of this passage is love "keeps no record of wrongs." Jesus died for our sins, and Jesus took away the sin of the world. I don't need to feel guilty about anything. I just get to experience my life because my life is a gift. It is a gift of grace. I've studied and done a lot of reading over the years, but that's what it's boiled down to for me. If I could just

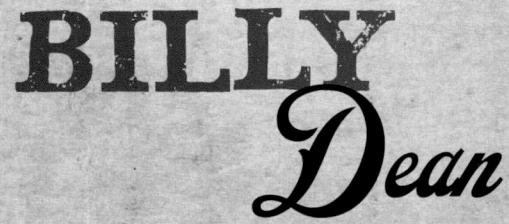

learn to be like that, to not hold any record of wrongs and to love unconditionally, I would be more God-like. I think that's what it's all about. Then everything falls into place. Your marriage falls into place when you do that. Parenting falls into place. Love is sufficient.

JASON *Crabb*

Trust in the LORD with all your heart and lean not on your own understanding; in all your ways submit to him, and he will make your paths straight. PROVERBS 3:5–6

When I started in the music world, I was singing with my family in a group. Everything looked so difficult to us … so hard. Success seemed an impossible goal to reach. We didn't know what to do or how to do it. We felt compelled that our music and ministry was who we were and that this was what our lives were supposed to entail, but it was often overwhelming. Those beginning points that happen in life are always the toughest.

Proverbs 3:5–6 is one of the Scriptures that I kept coming back to during those times. It's a passage I still go back to today when I have questions or face tough situations. When people ask me how I got started, I think of these verses. God has plans for us and we've got big dreams, and that takes me back to the source of what it's all about—trusting him.

I talk to so many people night after night at my concerts who are going through things and asking the same questions I have asked, such as, Which way do I turn? Or they say, I'm going through this or facing that. I always go back to Proverbs. Being married to Shellye, living the ups and downs of our lives, going through personal hard times and even traveling so much on the road, we've learned to realize that this difficulty, whatever it is at the moment, is not the end. During those times, we've always gone back to this Scripture as a couple. We have peace knowing we are really trying to live this Scripture out, doing our best to follow his direction and purpose and will for our lives.

KIMBERLY *Schlapman*

(LITTLE BIG TOWN)

Bear with each other and forgive one another if any of you has a grievance against someone. Forgive as the Lord forgave you. And over all these virtues put on love, which binds them all together in perfect unity. Let the peace of Christ rule in your hearts, since as members of one body you were called to peace. And be thankful.
COLOSSIANS 3:13–15

I have so many favorite Bible verses for different blessings and challenges in my life. But these verses seem to apply in every circumstance. Forgiveness is a gift to the forgiven as well as to the one who forgives. It offers freedom to both sides. Real love forgives and tries to forget.

I love these lines in particular: "Over all these virtues put on love . . . let the peace of Christ rule in your hearts." He says "over all." That seems pretty important. I believe real love brings forgiveness, which brings peace. Can you imagine how our tormented world would change if we all showed love and forgiveness even when we didn't feel like it? Most of the time, love breeds love. It's contagious. That's the kind of epidemic we need!

Living a life of love and peace and forgiveness and thanksgiving is so much less stressful than holding on to the resentment of being wronged. I try to be thankful in everything. God has shown me that he keeps me in the palm of his hand no matter the circumstance. I like being there.

LEE *Brice*

Be still, and know that I am God; I will be exalted among the nations, I will be exalted in the earth. PSALM 46:10

I have always loved this verse, and I even wrote a song about it called "Still." Tim McGraw recorded it and put it on the radio a few years ago. As time has gone by, that verse has come to mean even more to me, especially in my life right now. Everything moves so fast. My life was in high gear before, but it's in higher gear now. Sometimes it's hard to slow down and be still and talk to God and let him be a part of your life, but I try to make time. Every year I go camping in South Carolina with my two best friends and my brother. We go out in the swamp and disappear and nobody can find us for about four days and three nights. That's an important time for me. There are no phones, and there's nothing like that in the whole world. That's where I stop and take time to be still.

PHOTO: SHERRI GEORGE

DOYLE
Lawson

(DOYLE LAWSON & QUICKSILVER)

For it is by grace you have been saved, through faith—and this is not from yourselves, it is the gift of God. EPHESIANS 2:8

By God's grace, we can work and do all the good things, but Jesus said no man comes to the Father except through him. If you haven't accepted Jesus as your Savior, all the good things that you've done are for naught. It's by God's grace that he provided a way for us, sacrificing his only Son that we might have life. That's his grace.

In this life, it's not what you do materially. Things are material. They are short-lived. We go through this life and we have all good things. Believe me, I've been blessed far beyond belief for me, but those are just things. When God calls your number, all those things that you've received here will be left here, but if I've done something good in his name, for him, that won't be left here. It goes with me.

42

"Those Crazy Christians." I have a song on my album **Wheelhouse** by this title. The song is written from the point of view of someone baffled by people of faith. Most puzzling to the skeptic in the song is not the faith itself, but the actions that such faith produces. Things such as mission trips to dangerous regions, baptism, hospital visits to strangers, sobriety, forgiveness of atrocities, talk of heaven, etc., all must look insane to someone who is agnostic. But there is something so inspiring about watching believers do good things. Growing up in a small church, this was what stuck with me. That's why James 2:17 resonates with me.

The most impactful examples of someone's faith in action that I can remember aren't hands raised in the air, or shouts of hallelujah and joy, or judgment. It's the church members gathered around my cousin's bedside as he breathed his last, and how they took shifts 'round the clock with his family in those last two weeks while he fought for his life and lost.

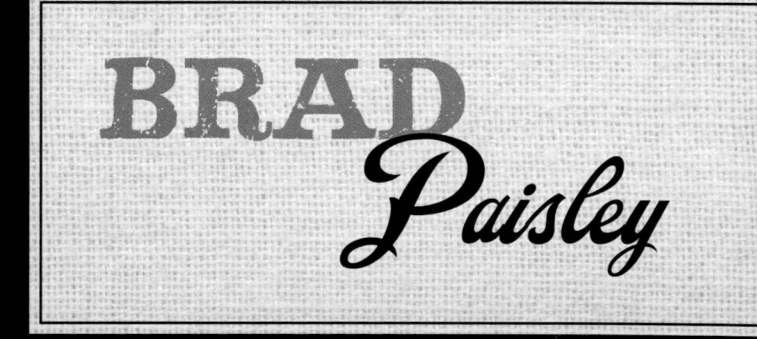

It's the Vanderpool family, who donate the majority of their income and time to charity. It's my wife, who found the same fire in fighting for the cause of relief in Haiti, taking multiple trips there to nurse the sick and the poor.

These are the people who inspire me. Not someone telling me how they think it is. No scare tactic or fire and brimstone sermon ever did diddly-squat to strengthen my faith. It was the works

CHERRILL *Green*

(EDENS EDGE)

There was a time about a year ago when I was really kind of sad. I started going through some old hymns and one popped up that had Psalm 119:105 in it. It's one of my favorites and has always brought me comfort in rough times.

It's really easy to give God the glory when everything is going great. Sometimes it's good for us to pray for a little storm because it makes you dig in, do some soul searching and discover what you truly believe yourself and not just what you were told as a kid. It's good to have your own personal relationship with the Lord that you have spent the time doing the work on—and find those Scriptures that really tweak at your heart. Those are the things that you can carry with you and turn to when you do experience a storm. They'll remind you of that peace that surpasses all understanding that you are always trying to get back to when you are in the midst of something heavy.

PHOTO: JEREMY COWART

The Word became flesh and made his dwelling among us. We have seen his glory, the glory of the one and only Son, who came from the Father, full of grace and truth. JOHN 1:14

It's hard for me to pick just one favorite Scripture passage, but whenever someone asks me that question I always go back to John 1. The very beginning of the Gospel of John is my favorite because it's the most poetic of all the Gospels. Throughout the whole book of John, there's this poetic thread of trying to describe to the people who Christ was and is. He refers to Christ as the Word, and that's why I think it's so powerful. He was in the beginning with God, all things were made through him. It tells you that he was around since the beginning of time. In other words, Christ always was. It wasn't like at the creation of the world the heavenly father was doing his thing and then Jesus showed up.

John 1 explains who Jesus is and what his mission on earth was, but then it comes back to verse 14, which reads, "The Word became flesh and made his dwelling among us. We have seen his glory, the glory of the one and only Son, who came from the Father, full of grace and truth." To me, that's just about all you need to know. As a Christian, if you understand that passage right there, everything else just sort of makes sense, and I love that.

John 1 has always been my favorite part of the Bible. I think it's so beautiful. I guess it's because I love the written word, and I'm a songwriter at heart. I love great songs and the Gospel of John was written like a songwriter would have written it.

LARRY Gatlin

This is how the birth of Jesus the Messiah came about: His mother Mary was pledged to be married to Joseph, but before they came together, she was found to be pregnant through the Holy Spirit ... But he did not consummate their marriage until she gave birth to a son. And he gave him the name Jesus. MATTHEW 1:18,25

The children of Israel coming out of Egypt, that's cool. The Garden of Eden and the snake and the apple, the rib, all that's cool, but it's just prelude. David killing Goliath, the Red Sea parting, Joseph and his brothers, Solomon and his temple, all of that is just prelude. Without the first five chapters of Matthew, the rest of it is just a bunch of fighting and killing and fornicating. I'll read that too, but the deal is the first chapter in the book of Matthew. If we as Christians don't pay attention to that, the rest of the book doesn't make any sense.

I heard somebody say one time that the reason raising children is so difficult is because children don't come with a manual. Well, children do come with a manual. It's called the Holy Bible. If you teach a child in the way they should go, when they are old they will not depart from it. When they are 16 and 17 and it looks like they are going against it, they will come back because it's a promise in the Word of God. He gave us a manual of how to live.

49

WYNONNA

Do not be anxious about anything, but in every situation, by prayer and petition, with thanksgiving, present your requests to God. And the peace of God, which transcends all understanding, will guard your hearts and your minds in Christ Jesus. PHILIPPIANS 4:6–7

The peace of God that surpasses all understanding is what I constantly search for as a believer. When I'm feeling anxious and/or afraid, in pain or in times where I am experiencing darkness, I have found it helps to slow down, concentrate on my breathing and say "in with peace" as I inhale. Then I say, "out with fear" or whatever it is that I am feeling in that moment as I exhale. I find that in time, a peace washes over me. Though everything may not be okay, I am okay with everything because I truly feel a sense of peace and calm that allows me to continue my belief that "this too shall pass."

It has taken me a lifetime to get to where I am today. I can—with my whole heart—say that Philippians 4:6–7 has come true in my life and has helped me to walk through the toughest of times.

DANNY *Gokey*

We live in a world where we see so many terrible things, tragedies and trials. Sometimes the floor can drop out right underneath us. When my first wife passed away, I essentially thought that life was over. I started thinking that God didn't like me. When I found Jeremiah 29:11, that verse changed everything. I found that he does have a good plan. Even though this terrible thing had happened, he still had a plan for my life. My life wasn't over like I thought it was. He had a plan for my life, and it was actually better than I ever thought it could be. God has an expectation for me that I'm going to fulfill this good plan that he has for me. The moment we change our thinking and start connecting with God, we start connecting with his plans, which always exceed our small plans.

Sometimes bad things can condition our minds to think that God is not on our side, but this verse reminds us that God does care. There's hope. In my life, I've experienced some pretty difficult things. When trials hit, our minds always wants to ask, "Where is God? Why isn't he stopping this?" Sometimes we think, "Does he not like me? Is he against me?" And then we open the Bible to Jeremiah 29:11, and it totally tells the truth. The truth is that God has good things for us. He has a plan. Even before we stepped on this earth, he had a plan for our lives. I find that very comforting.

JOHN Berry

For God so loved the world that he gave his one and only Son, that whoever believes in him shall not perish but have eternal life. JOHN 3:16

When I was a little boy, my mom led me to the Lord. The day it all went down I came home from school, and she was sitting on the porch reading a book. I went out there and, like all little fellows who have a lot to say but don't know exactly what to say, I sort of shuffled my feet around and my mama said; "What's on your mind? Johnny come here."

I sat on the swing next to her. She put her arm around me and pulled me all up close to her and said, "You tell your momma what's on your mind." I said, "They've been teaching me stuff in Sunday school, and I've been thinking about it so much. About Jesus dying on a cross, his blood being shed and then rising from the dead, going to heaven and coming back. There's a holy ghost involved, and it scares me to death." She laughed and said, "It's the greatest story ever told."

She opened up the Bible and shared some verses with me and explained them in a way I could really understand. But the one verse that meant the most to me was John 3:16. She read it and said, "Look right here! It says, 'For God so loves Johnny, that he gave his only begotten son, that if Johnny believes in him, Johnny will have everlasting life.'" I could get that. My little nine-and-a-half-year-old mind couldn't get that whole world thing, but the fact that God loved me enough that he sent Jesus for ME! I could get that.

Blessed is the one whose transgressions are forgiven, whose sins are covered. PSALM 32:1

Psalm 32:1 has always meant a great deal to me because it's about forgiveness. Many times people are embarrassed about things they've done that are sins against God and their faith. They are afraid to recognize that it's important to wash that sin away by acknowledging what they've done. We do that through repentance and our relationship with God.

In our lives we are extremely transparent today with the kind of media coverage that we have, particularly the social media. Before I met my wife, my sins were quite evident. Fortunately we didn't have the kind of transparency we have now because the things I did that were either a sin against my ex-wives or in my personal life, I was just really embarrassed about. So when we talk about the kind of forgiveness we get, particularly in Psalm 32, we acknowledge our sin and then the burden is off our shoulders. We have to come to the realization that Jesus Christ died on the cross to relieve us of that burden. I think once we recognize his sacrifice, it's so much easier to go through life and forgive others.

LEE Greenwood

I have signed Mark 10:45 next to my name for as long as I've been signing autographs. I want my name be tied to the Word of God. When folks see my signature, I want that verse to always be there because I don't want any separation between me and my love for God and his Word.

Mark 10:45 is a life verse that has essentially the gospel wrapped up in it—the Good News of the reason Jesus came. He came to ransom mankind. It says, first of all, that mankind needed ransom, that we were held captive by sin. It's through his death that forgiveness came. I love that word ransom because it's easy to understand, especially in our movie-going culture. There's always a good movie on that has that component to it. The good guys have to figure out how to get their loved ones back. It's interesting that even those who have not yet found Jesus still rally around those themes that Jesus modeled perfectly, including ransoming mankind.

The way we are to serve those around us is as he did. All through Scripture that's what he does. He serves mankind. He is King of kings and Lord of lords, yet we find him washing the disciples' feet. We find him healing the sick, the lame, the blind. We find him feeding the hungry and giving a drink to the woman at the well when no one else would. He's the ultimate servant. For me, the whole gospel is wrapped up in that poignant, powerful verse.

GUY
Penrod

SCOTTY McCreery

I can do all this through him who gives me strength.
PHILIPPIANS 4:13

Philippians 4:13 has been my verse since I was a kid. I keep a lot of my old baseball hats, and if you look in the hats I've had since I started pitching, you'll see Philippians 4:13 written on the brim. That's the Scripture that gets me through the day because sometimes you can't do it all by yourself. You can't do it on your own, so you lean on him. That's what's gotten me through life.

This was especially true during my time on *American Idol*. For 16 years, all I knew was wake up, go see my friends at school, come back home and chill. Then all of a sudden I'm in Los Angeles, in the hustle and bustle of a big city on a TV show in front of millions. It was the best time of my life, but it was tough and definitely stressful. That was when I'd have to really dig into the Word and pray and ask for prayers from my friends back home. I leaned on that verse, and I got through it. The reason I think I'm where I'm at now is because it's my purpose. Every day when I'm by myself playing the guitar, I thank God. Or if I'm on an awards show or a TV show getting recognized, I thank him and let people hear about it.

MIRANDA *Lambert*

A wife of noble character is her husband's crown. PROVERBS 12:4

Going through the problems that you go through your first year of marriage, people say it's the hardest year, and it was difficult. We had a lot of loss in our first year with [my husband] Blake's dad passing away and my childhood friend passing away and being apart. With Blake being on the TV show *The Voice* and me on tour, there were a lot of ups and downs. I just realized how important the sanctity of marriage is, how much we needed each other, and how good it feels to know somebody has your back.

Proverbs 12:4 really means something to me. I love it. I thought about getting a tattoo of it because I want to always know that it's there. More than any diamond or anything else, it's really tattooed on my heart.

KENI *Thomas*

Then I heard the voice of the Lord saying, "Whom shall I send? And who will go for us?" And I said, "Here am I. Send me!" ISAIAH 6:8

Every morning at zero dark thirty somewhere around this globe, men from the 75th Ranger Regiment are standing in formation starting their day by screaming out the six stanzas of the Ranger Creed. The point of saying a creed every day is to commit it to memory. When you say something enough, you begin to believe it. When you believe it, you will live it.

I don't know if you have a creed you live by. But if you need one, I've got one for you—Isaiah 6:8. It's on the walls of the 75th Ranger Regiment in Ft. Benning, Ga. In fact, it's on the walls of every special operations unit out there. I remember the first time I read that Scripture. It was on the wall at the US Army's Delta Force compound in Ft. Bragg, NC. I thought, "Hmm, *send me*. That dude Isaiah must have been a soldier! Because *send me* was an easy thing for us to say. Give me the job! Let me go do what I've been training to do. Let me make my difference in this world." That was then. This is now. I don't get to carry an M-4 rifle anymore. I do, however, get to carry a guitar. Both have a working end. Both can make an impact, either positively or negatively.

I can tell a story. I can sing a song. It is a gift I have been given. And with that gift, I will once again raise my hand to God and ask him to send me. I will use the opportunity to tell people that they are extraordinary individuals and that they too have a chance to be sent to make a difference in this world, starting with the people on their left and on their right.

Where are you being sent? Who are you impacting and how? Who are you leading? Who are you following? How are you making a difference? It all begins by raising your hand and stepping up. Here I am, Lord. Send me.

The ROYS

(ELAINE AND LEE ROY)

The LORD has done it this very day; let us rejoice today and be glad. PSALM 118:24

This verse has the power to change our lives if we really take a moment to look at what we are reading. Every day that we are granted is a chance to begin again, a fresh start. We have all had those days when we have lost hope or nothing seems to be going right. If we could take a moment in those days of desperation and stop to look around us, we would see God's painting staring back at us. Just being in nature and hearing birds singing or watching the colors of the leaves change in the fall, viewing a sunset or a sunrise—it's all amazing. He has made that day for each one of us to rejoice in.

Life is so hectic, and with cell phones and computers it's hard to disconnect these days. There just seems to be no time left to rejoice in the day. We need to stop and take in those simple yet powerful moments that pass so quickly, because in an instant things change. It means appreciating everything and everyone in our lives and to always thank God in all of it. He knows the plans he has for us, and they are good. Life is precious— we need to rejoice in it!

RAY Stevens

And we know that in all things God works for the good of those who love him, who have been called according to his purpose. ROMANS 8:28

We were Southern Baptist, and my mama was a Sunday school teacher. I got up every Sunday morning, put on my best clothes and got on down there to church. There are a lot of Scriptures that mean a great deal to me, and one I've always liked is Romans 8:28. It says, "All things God works for the good of those who love him, who have been called according to his purpose." To me, that means as we deal with the many pressures of life, it takes faith and trust and patience. I believe in regard to some things we'll have to wait and see the ultimate good after we have entered the next world, but I'll bet everybody who is already there can see everything very clearly.

I have wondered if I haven't really messed up at times, but I was doing what I thought was the right thing, and it has all worked out. In the next life, I'm sure I'll see the ultimate fruition of what I didn't realize in this life. As a believer, you've got to be trusting and faithful.

JOEY Martin Feek

But if serving the LORD seems undesirable to you, then choose for yourselves this day whom you will serve, whether the gods your ancestors served beyond the Euphrates, or the gods of the Amorites, in whose land you are living. But as for me and my household, we will serve the LORD. JOSHUA 24:15

The verse that hits home the most to me is Joshua 24:15, especially the line, "...as for me and my household, we will serve the LORD." Even though Rory and I get to travel all over the country singing, I love being at home at our farmhouse. I love cooking and cleaning and taking care of my home and my family. I try hard to be a good wife and a good mother to our girls. It's not always easy, but it's so important. That verse reminds me that when I'm loving and serving others, I'm actually serving God. And that, above everything else, is what I truly strive to do. God has been so good to me, and I never want to forget that this day and this moment is a blessing from God.

RORY Feek

Reaching into his bag and taking out a stone, [David] slung it and struck the Philistine on the forehead. The stone sank into his forehead, and he fell facedown on the ground. 1 SAMUEL 17:49

My favorite verse is 1 Samuel 17:49. I've always believed that anything is possible. Even as a little kid, I dreamed big and believed those dreams could come true. I had no real reason to believe that they would. I'd never really been around anyone else whose dreams had come true, but I still believed. When I grew up and became a Christian, that belief only became stronger.

Sometimes the obstacles in our lives seem too enormous to overcome or the odds are clearly stacked against us. But like David when he faced Goliath, with God on our side the impossible becomes very possible. I have seen and felt God move mountains in my life again and again. And when he does, I can only drop to my knees in humility, knowing that it wasn't me who "slayed the giant." It was God. It's always God.

ALAN *Jackson*

And now these three remain: faith, hope and love. But the greatest of these is love. 1 CORINTHIANS 13:13

Honestly, I can't choose a single favorite Bible verse. But one verse that is right up there at the top of my list is one I've sort of become known for—1 Corinthians 13:13. While I've always loved this verse, one night in October of 2001, I woke up in the middle of the night with the words to that verse in my head. I got up immediately and wrote, "Where Were You (When the World Stopped Turning)," which is a song that tries to process some of the grief America was experiencing after the September 11th attacks. It is a simple song, but because it's based on 1 Corinthians 13:13, I'm not surprised that it has brought comfort to millions of people. I can't tell you how many people have shared with me where they were when they first heard that song, and how it touched them. I didn't really write the song, I just held the pen—this song was truly a gift from God.

DARIUS *Rucker*

A cheerful heart is good medicine, but a crushed spirit dries up the bones. PROVERBS 17:22

"A cheerful heart is good medicine, but a crushed spirit dries up the bones." That's how I live my life, to be happy and make other people feel happy and uplifted. That was one of those things I heard when I was a kid growing up in Charleston, SC. My mom told me to always be nice to people. She shared a lot of other Scriptures with me, but that one always stuck with me.

We were church-going people. My mom was very, very religious, and to always be good was something she instilled in me as a kid. It was one of those things I remembered. Proverbs 17:22 is so vivid in what it's saying. For me, I got it and that's how I try to live my life. I think that's the way many of us try to live our lives—just try to be happy and make sure you're not trying to make anybody else unhappy. Today everybody seems so divided about one thing or another, whether it's music or politics or whatever. I think if we had more people bringing light to other people's lives, the world would be a better place.

The LORD is my shepherd, I lack nothing.
  He makes me lie down in green pastures,
he leads me beside quiet waters,
  he refreshes my soul.
He guides me along the right paths
  for his name's sake.
Even though I walk
  through the darkest valley,
I will fear no evil,
  for you are with me;
your rod and your staff,
  they comfort me.

You prepare a table before me
  in the presence of my enemies.
You anoint my head with oil;
  my cup overflows.
Surely your goodness and love will follow me
  all the days of my life,
and I will dwell in the house of the LORD
  forever. PSALM 23

Psalm 23 fits every generation and everything that happens in our life. There's nothing I shall want, and as long as he is my shepherd, I know he's going to take care of me. As we get older we appreciate the Scriptures a lot more, especially during trials and ups and downs in life. When I think about the death of my father when I was 16 and the death of my husband Keith [Whitley], it was my faith that got me through. I got through those hard times because of my faith, my friends and my family. I think what's missing in our society is that people today are walking away from faith. To me, it's something I hang on to and lean on. I'm a big Mike Huckabee fan, and I heard him say on TV that people are always asking, "How could God let this happen?" He said that God didn't let this happen, but unfortunately we are pushing God out of schools and only calling on him when bad things happen. We need to have him there as a priority again.

HUNTER *Hayes*

In you, LORD my God,
  I put my trust.

I trust in you;
  do not let me be put to shame,
  nor let my enemies triumph over me.
No one who hopes in you
  will ever be put to shame,
but shame will come on those
  who are treacherous without cause.

Show me your ways, LORD,
  teach me your paths.
Guide me in your truth and teach me,
  for you are God my Savior,
  and my hope is in you all day long.
PSALM 25:1–5

I connect with many things in the Psalms because this book is so poetic and so musical. It is a series of lyrics about life, faith, the good times and bad times, and the realistic struggles and triumphs through faith in words that are timeless and truthful. It's as if I can relate to this book much like I do to music. I have said many times that music is the soundtrack to my life, and I feel like some verses from Psalms could very well be the stories of my own faith.

I love Psalm 25:1–5. These specific verses basically sum up what is my prayer. Specifically, "Show me your ways, LORD teach me your paths" and "in you, LORD my God, I put my trust." That is to say it brings me back to what's important in the faith I have. I feel these verses are honest, passionate, profound and reflective.

PHOTO: JARRETT GAZA

If my people, who are called by my name, will humble themselves and pray and seek my face and turn from their wicked ways, then I will hear from heaven, and I will forgive their sin and will heal their land.
2 CHRONICLES 7:14

There are so many great verses in the Bible. It's difficult to pick just one, but I chose 2 Chronicles 7:14 because of the way things are in our nation today. It seems that everywhere we turn people are trying to take God out of our country, out of our lives—steering us away from him and the principles upon which our great country was founded. Yet, as this verse tells us, there is hope. If we put God back into our lives, he will heal our land.

RICHARD *Sterban*

(THE OAK RIDGE BOYS)

The Oak Ridge Boys try to include gospel music whenever, wherever we perform because we want to remind people to think about God and his promises. As a result, we hope we can play a part in helping turn our nation back to him.

We are often asked to sing the national anthem at sporting and civic events. One of my favorite stanzas isn't largely known, but it speaks eloquently of the relationship between our country and our God:

O, thus be it ever when freemen shall stand,
Between their lov'd home and the war's desolation.
Blest with vict'ry and peace, may the heav'n-rescued land
Praise the Pow'r that hath made and preserv'd us a nation!
Then conquer we must, when our cause is just,
And this be our motto: "In God is our trust."
And the star-spangled banner in triumph shall wave
O'er the land of the free and the home of the brave!

DUANE *Allen*

(THE OAK RIDGE BOYS)

Then the King will say to those on his right, "Come, you who are blessed by my Father; take your inheritance, the kingdom prepared for you since the creation of the world. For I was hungry and you gave me something to eat, I was thirsty and you gave me something to drink, I was a stranger and you invited me in." MATTHEW 25:34–35

I do much of my personal work for charity in private because I am not looking for applause. My reason for doing so comes from the teachings in Matthew. I learned a lot about giving at an early age from my father. It was known throughout our house that we Allen children could not have our Christmas until we had shared our food and Christmas gifts with a "needy" family in our community. This was quite a lesson to learn to live out as a child. Therefore, this verse inspires my caring for those less fortunate among us. I try to live by this Scripture in my charity work, in my family and in my group.

PHOTO: JONATHAN EXLEY

BARBARA *Mandrell*

And we know that in all things God works for the good of those who love him, who have been called according to his purpose.
ROMANS 8:28

I remember telling my uncle Ira one day that my favorite Scripture verse is Romans 8:28. I said, "All things happen for the good for those who love the Lord." He said, "Go on." I repeated, "Romans 8:28, All things happen for the good for those who love the Lord." He asked me to finish the rest of the verse, and I said, "and are living according to his purpose." He said, "There you go! That's what makes it special!"

God has shown me a couple of things through this Scripture, which I refer to in my mind and heart many, many times when I have disappointments, heartaches and difficulties. It's very hard to stay in the joy of the Lord when you're disappointed. It's very, very hard, but no matter how bad, how tragic, how horrible, that Scripture reminds me it's happening for the good because I love God. And, while I'm not always doing it right, I'm attempting to live according to his purposes.

Romans 8:28 helps me to gain strength because if you have your personal relationship with God and it's a real relationship, he guides you. He directs you. He makes it all good. And, of course, it's true yesterday, today and forever.

The BAND PERRY

(KIMBERLY, REID AND NEIL PERRY)

Consider it pure joy, my brothers and sisters, whenever you face trials of many kinds, because you know that the testing of your faith produces perseverance. Let perseverance finish its work so that you may be mature and complete, not lacking anything.   JAMES 1:2–4

This verse has been our guiding light over the last 14 years and has carried us through many late nights and the blood, sweat and tears. There have been so many times along the way when one of us wanted to give up because there seemed like no way to keep plowing forward, but that Scripture constantly reminded us what we were created to do, so we persevered.

These verses also say trials make you complete and prepare you for your life's work, and we certainly think the three of us were prepared for this moment. It's interesting because we were pretty much in complete anonymity for about the first 12 years of our journey. We do feel like it was all those long hours and sometimes discouraging moments that prepared us to be in the spotlight. We're still learning so much every day and will as long as we're on the planet, but we do feel prepared as human beings and as artists for this moment.

GENE *Watson*

Therefore, as God's chosen people, holy and dearly loved, clothe yourselves with compassion, kindness, humility, gentleness and patience. COLOSSIANS 3:12

I've always believed strongly in the Golden Rule: "Do to others what you would have them do to you" (Matthew 7:12). This verse from Colossians is one of my favorites because it speaks to that teaching. I've always tried to live by the Golden Rule and to treat people with kindness and fairness. It's a teaching that was passed down in my large family from my parents to all my brothers and sisters. There were seven of us kids, and we learned early on from our parents that we needed to share and to be kind to one another. We grew up poor, living in an old school bus my dad fixed up for us so we could travel from job to job, but my parents always made time on Sundays for us to attend church. They never let us forget these important words from the Bible. Even though sometimes I get low or out of sorts, I still try to have patience and to show respect and compassion for those around me.

JIMMY *Wayne*

Religion that God our Father accepts as pure and faultless is this: to look after orphans and widows in their distress and to keep oneself from being polluted by the world. JAMES 1:27

When I first read the book of James, I fell in love with this verse. It says true religion is to care for the orphans and widows. It's telling us what we are supposed to be doing. It doesn't say you have to take a kid into your home. It doesn't say you have to donate money. It says care for them however you can, the best you can. A guy I know owns a guitar company and has the ability and resources to donate 25 guitars to a youth facility. He's caring for the orphans by doing that. It might be writing a song that speaks up for the orphans. If songwriting is your resource, that's how you can care for them. There are people who donate money and that's good too. It keeps the lights on and the water bill paid, so we need all of these people.

When I was 16-years-old and homeless, there was a wonderful couple, Bea and Russell Costner, who took me in and changed my life. At Bea's funeral, I remember looking out over the congregation and seeing some other kids they had helped. They'd been taking in kids their entire adult lives. They were doing exactly what it says in James 1:27. I've tried to carry on their legacy. In 2010 I walked from Nashville to Phoenix to bring attention to the plight of children who age out of the foster care system, and I've worked to pass legislation that helps these kids. For eight years, I've spent time with the youth at Nashville's Monroe Harding children's home. It really means a lot to me. I enjoy that way more than I do playing on any stage. I played Madison Square Garden and that was cool, but whose life was changed? When I go someplace like Monroe Harding, and I'm sitting in a conference room with 25 kids, there are no spotlights. I'm just doing what I do, and it's so much more fulfilling to me.

PHOTO: GLEN ROSE

But the fruit of the Spirit is love, joy, peace, forbearance, kindness, goodness, faithfulness, gentleness and self-control. Against such things there is no law. GALATIANS 5:22–23

I feel like I have my own connection with the man above. My father is a deacon at a church in Fort Worth, Texas. He and my mom are very heavily involved in church, and I've been trying to find my own way with it all. I've got great friends who are Jewish. I've got a lot of friends who are Christian like myself. I've got good friends who are Southern Baptist and Catholic. It's all across the board. One of the Scriptures that means the most to me is Galatians 5:22–23. I feel like this Scripture is universal. Everyone believes in those things, no matter if you are a Christian or if you practice Judaism. Everyone believes in those things. The funny thing is that none of us can actually live up to the challenge of always bearing those fruits. But I try to live my life by showing patience, being kind, having goodness and faithfulness and self-control, which are things that we all as human beings can live by.

JT *Hodges*

NEAL McCoy

Here I am! I stand at the door and knock. If anyone hears my voice and opens the door, I will come in and eat with that person, and they with me. REVELATION 3:20

The thing I like about this verse is the simplicity. God is saying, "I'm here. I'm knocking. If you open the door, I'll come be with you." It's up to us to let him into our lives, to open the door. It's pretty basic, and it really touches me because I've opened the door.

I was baptized at 13-years-old at the First Christian Church in Jacksonville, Texas. It's the church I grew up in. I know that is when I was supposed to have turned my life over to the Lord, but I don't know if it's always that simple. Some kids go to revivals, get caught up in the moment and get baptized. To tell you the truth, in my case, I'm not sure that that's when it happened. I sure felt good about it when I was doing it. It felt like the right thing to do, but I know from then on, I went and sinned. I know we are forgiven of our sins, but it took me until a little later in life to understand what I had in life. When I had a wife and kids, I came to understand what life was really about and really appreciate what I had with my career and family.

So although I did get baptized and saved when I was young, I'm not sure that I really understood what I was doing. Some people might say it's not right to say that, but I think that's right for me. When I did open the door, I know that I may not have opened it all at one time. I might have opened it a little bit and God got a foot in. He stayed and kept knocking until eventually I did open the door, and he came all the way in. I just opened it a little bit at a time. I know he's in now, and that's the most important thing.

JAMIE O'Neal

I have told you these things, so that in me you may have peace. In this world you will have trouble. But take heart! I have overcome the world. JOHN 16:33

In this life we all deal with "issues." As I'm sure many people have, so many times I have asked, "Why is this happening to me? Or How do I move on past this?" Pain, grief and loss have affected us all. In 2000 my grandfather, whom I was close to, had stomach cancer. At the same time, my grandmother had Alzheimer's. This coincided with my wedding and the release of my first CD. The pain and fear I felt about losing my grandparents and starting a new chapter of my life knowing that they wouldn't be here to see it was excruciating. I can still feel the grief today.

However, my grandfather—Siggi, as I called him—always spoke about God and having faith in our higher power. He never in his entire life complained or asked, "Why me?" My grandparents and my parents have always strongly believed there is no separation even after death, and that gave me comfort when they passed away. Just like they are always with me, so is God—leading us through the ups and downs, the triumphs and tribulations.

The only thing that gets me through hard times is the knowledge that Jesus has "overcome the world," as it says in John 16:33. God never leaves us, and having faith in him is what comforts me. It gives me peace knowing I can turn everything over to him.

But Jesus went to the Mount of Olives. At dawn he appeared again in the temple courts, where all the people gathered around him, and he sat down to teach them. The teachers of the law and the Pharisees brought in a woman caught in adultery. They made her stand before the group and said to Jesus, "Teacher, this woman was caught in the act of adultery. In the Law Moses commanded us to stone such women. Now what do you say?" They were using this question as a trap, in order to have a basis for accusing him. But Jesus bent down and started to write on the ground with his finger. When they kept on questioning him, he straightened up and said to them, "Let any one of you who is without sin be the first to throw a stone at her." Again he stooped down and wrote on the ground. At this, those who heard began to go away one at a time, the older ones first, until only Jesus was left, with the woman still standing there. Jesus straightened up and asked her, "Woman, where are they? Has no one condemned you?" "No one, sir," she said. "Then neither do I condemn you," Jesus declared. "Go now and leave your life of sin."
JOHN 8:1–11

I have always thought John 8:1–11 was pretty cool. I love it because it's the truth. We've all made mistakes. We're all sinners saved by grace. We all fall short of who we should be, but that's just the deal. Only one perfect human has walked the earth. However, everybody is always so quick to judge each other and point out the faults in other people. The truth is that we've all sinned. If you think you are better than someone else or haven't sinned, you really need to take a look inside yourself. We are all sinners, and we shouldn't judge others. I like verse 7 because it teaches compassion and forgiveness, "Let any one of you who is without sin be the first to throw a stone at her." And no one did. Nobody can say that they haven't sinned.

PHIL *Vassar*

PHOTO: KRISTIN BARLOWE

CRAIG *Morgan*

No one will be able to stand against you. The LORD your God, as he promised you, will put the terror and fear of you on the whole land, wherever you go. DEUTERONOMY 11:25

I have this verse tattooed on my arm. I've had it a while and the reason is because I firmly believe that if you have enough confidence in faith and belief in your Lord, then even death itself will not stop you. It's the only tattoo I have, and it's wrapped around me. The entire verse goes around my tricep and bicep and there's a big cross on my arm. It represents me living my life to the very extreme. Everyone that knows me knows that I live extremely fast. I work hard, and I always play hard too [hunting, fishing and racing BMX motorbikes].

Some would say that it's not very Christian of me and I should take better care of myself, but I know that my God wants me to love my life and love my family and friends and do everything I can to worship him. That's what I've focused on more than anything else in the last 15 years of my life. I don't worry about everything else around me as much as I concentrate on my relationship with him. It's funny because when you do that and you are really focused on your relationship with him, everything else falls completely into place, including your witness.

PHOTO: KRISTIN BARLOWE

FLORIDA GEORGIA
Line

BRIAN KELLEY

"For I know the plans I have for you," declares the LORD, "plans to prosper you and not to harm you, plans to give you hope and a future."
JEREMIAH 29:11

That's been a favorite verse of mine since I was young. My parents used to read this to me before our bedtime prayers every night, and I remember hearing it often in Sunday school. It just stuck with me and continues to inspire me to work hard and do what I love—play, write and breathe music.

I always knew deep down that if I stayed the course and walked with the Lord, he would be there to guide me through, even during the most difficult times when Tyler [Hubbard] and I did everything we possibly could—hung drywall, detailed cars—to make ends meet. We always kept our focus on the goal of music. To me, the words of Jeremiah 29:11 provide comfort and fortitude in the challenging times we face in our lives, along with knowing the Lord is looking out for us and protecting us along the way. It's an awesome and inspiring verse that has helped lead me to where I am today.

TYLER HUBBARD

But those who hope in the LORD will renew their strength. They will soar on wings like eagles; they will run and not grow weary, they will walk and not be faint. ISAIAH 40:31

This was actually my dad's favorite Bible verse, and he instilled a lot of it into me. I think it goes to show no matter what we go through—hard times, good times—walk with the Lord and he'll give you the strength to get through whatever life throws at you. That's important to remember because even when things are going great, there's going to be the hard times in life. Brian [Kelley] and I get exhausted. As great as this life is and as great as everything is going, there are times that are really exhausting and you have to find your strength in the Lord.

PHOTO: KRISTIN BARLOWE

There is a time for everything,
  and a season for every activity under the heavens:
  a time to be born and a time to die,
  a time to plant and a time to uproot,
  a time to kill and a time to heal,
  a time to tear down and a time to build,
  a time to weep and a time to laugh,
  a time to mourn and a time to dance,
  a time to scatter stones and a time to gather them,
  a time to embrace and a time to refrain from embracing,
  a time to search and a time to give up,
  a time to keep and a time to throw away,
  a time to tear and a time to mend,
  a time to be silent and a time to speak,
  a time to love and a time to hate,
  a time for war and a time for peace.
ECCLESIASTES 3:1–8

JOANNA Smith

Amidst all of the Bible's lofty language, this is a poem for the working man—for all of us. It is powerful not in an angel's singing in heaven kind of a way, but in a Jesus on earth kind of way. It's the page I turn to when my life feels off kilter, I can't find the right answer, or I've tried hard to live up to an ideal and have failed. It acknowledges the gray area in life. When I read it, I feel God saying he knows what I'm going through. It teaches me that each day is its own day. There aren't any programs, any guarantees. And, therefore, it teaches me to live by faith one moment at a time, and to trust that I'll be prepared for each one as it comes.

After reading this verse, I can no longer judge another. While it may have been my time to weep, it may have been their time to laugh. While it may have been my time to plant, it may have been their time to uproot. It gives me peace in patience. For everything, there is a time. Life has many struggles. This is a fallen world, but I find comfort in knowing there's a great God out there who understands.

PHOTO: ANTHONY LADD

MARTY *Raybon*

Trust in the LORD with all your heart and lean not on your own understanding; in all your ways submit to him, and he will make your paths straight. PROVERBS 3:5–6

A couple of years ago I was diagnosed with prostate cancer. I'd been going to the doctor since I was 45-years-old because my dad, my grandfather and two of my uncles died of prostate cancer. If we don't think that our life can change in an instant, then we're sadly mistaken. It can be going to the doctor and hearing the words "you've got cancer" or getting a telephone call that says "your child has been in a car accident." Our life can change literally in an instant, and those are the times we need our faith and our trust in him.

Only the Lord has the answers to our questions in life. Why did the tornado hit that house? Why did that baby have to die? Why did that woman get cancer? Faith is the most important thing that anybody could ever have. God really wants us to trust him. When bad things happen, we may not know why. We don't know the answers, but God does and we just have to trust him with all our heart.

CHARLIE *Daniels*

"Because he loves me," says the LORD, "I will rescue him;
  I will protect him, for he acknowledges my name.
He will call on me, and I will answer him;
  I will be with him in trouble,
  I will deliver him and honor him.
With long life I will satisfy him
  and show him my salvation." PSALM 91:14–16

I committed to memory quite a while back Psalm 91. It's a psalm of trust, of safety, of leaning on God for your protection, of knowing that he is in charge. I like that. It doesn't make a difference what anybody else does or what happens with any other situation, you have protection over you. These are not just pretty poetic words. These are promises, and I committed them to memory. I do so much traveling, and I will say Psalm 91 to myself. I remember being in Iraq, and it meant a lot to me there to be able to say that psalm. I was definitely protected in Iraq. We got shot at when we were heading to a remote base to entertain the troops.

Psalm 91 is a comfort to me. It's just talking to God, saying I serve you and I believe in you. I know that you are taking care of me. It's a very special psalm to somebody who travels as much as I do. God protects us. Every breath and every heartbeat is a blessing from God. We tend to sometimes forget that the next breath we take is a gift. Every beat of our heart, every sight we see, every sound we hear, every note of music I write, sing or play is all a blessing from God. Psalm 91 is one of God's presents. It's saying, "I've got you, son. I've got you covered. You don't have to worry about that. Let me worry about that. You go ahead and do the best you can, and I'll take care of the rest."

SARA *Evans*

And we know that in all things God works for the good of those who love him, who have been called according to his purpose.
ROMANS 8:28

When I first met my husband, Jay, every time he would sign an autograph, he would sign: "Jay Barker Roll Tide! Romans 8:28." From the moment he started signing autographs, he decided to put that Bible verse because it's always been his favorite. It gives you hope. It is such a peace-giving verse.

Both of us went through a divorce, which was really tough. We were introduced to each other by a friend, and now we've been married for five years. We're blissfully happy and blissfully in love. All of it worked out for good. God was so merciful and gracious to us in letting us find each other and our children blending and becoming siblings. Everything at our wedding had Romans 8:28 printed on it. Our napkins said, "Jay and Sara, Romans 8:28," because it's so true for us.

In everything we went through we always stayed faithful to the Lord. We didn't blame him or ever question his love or faithfulness. Everything did eventually work all together for the good. That gives me such hope. No matter what happens in the future, we know that if we love the Lord then he is going to work it out for the good. It may not be exactly what we want or what we thought, but it's for our good because he knows what is best for us. He's already seen the end of everything and knows exactly what we need. Jay and I pray all the time for the Lord to remind us of that verse and also to remind us that he's going to meet all of our needs; not all of our wants, but he's going to meet all of our needs.

PHOTO: RUSS HARRINGTON

INTRODUCTION TO THE

Book OF MARK

Now that you've read all the reflections, it's your turn to ponder the question: What passage from the Bible is the most meaningful to you—and why? How do these verses inspire, encourage or motivate you?

To give you a helpful start in your quest for the answers to these questions, we've provided one of the Bible's 66 books—the Gospel of Mark. While it's the shortest of the four New Testament Gospels, Mark is definitely not short on action. Here, Jesus raises a dead girl, heals blind men, calms a raging storm with just three words, feeds 5,000 with five loaves of bread and two fish—and then walks on water to his disciples who were drowning in a sea of fear and doubt.

You'll find that the Gospel (which means "Good News") of Mark offers a straightforward, detailed account of Jesus' ministry, including many of his parables and miracles, and his death and resurrection—all packed into just 16 chapters. So, go ahead. Read and experience Mark at your own pace. Also consider using the hash tag #CountryFaith on Twitter or Facebook to share your favorite passage so that your friends will be encouraged to go deeper in their faith—wherever they are in the world.

After all, spreading the Good News is what *Once-a-Day Country Faith* is all about.

John the Baptist Prepares the Way

1 The beginning of the good news about Jesus the Messiah,[a] the Son of God,[b] [2]as it is written in Isaiah the prophet:

"I will send my messenger ahead of you,
    who will prepare your way"[c] —
[3]"a voice of one calling in the wilderness,
'Prepare the way for the Lord,
    make straight paths for him.'"[d]

[4]And so John the Baptist appeared in the wilderness, preaching a baptism of repentance for the forgiveness of sins. [5]The whole Judean countryside and all the people of Jerusalem went out to him. Confessing their sins, they were baptized by him in the Jordan River. [6]John wore clothing made of camel's hair, with a leather belt around his waist, and he ate locusts and wild honey. [7]And this was his message: "After me comes the one more powerful than I, the straps of whose sandals I am not worthy to stoop down and untie. [8]I baptize you with[e] water, but he will baptize you with[e] the Holy Spirit."

The Baptism and Testing of Jesus

[9]At that time Jesus came from Nazareth in Galilee and was baptized by John in the Jordan. [10]Just as Jesus was coming up out of the water, he saw heaven being torn open and the Spirit descending on him like a dove. [11]And a voice came from heaven: "You are my Son, whom I love; with you I am well pleased."

[12]At once the Spirit sent him out into the wilderness, [13]and he was in the wilderness forty days, being tempted[f] by Satan. He was with the wild animals, and angels attended him.

Jesus Announces the Good News

[14]After John was put in prison, Jesus went into Galilee, proclaiming the good news of God. [15]"The time has come," he said. "The kingdom of God has come near. Repent and believe the good news!"

Jesus Calls His First Disciples

[16]As Jesus walked beside the Sea of Galilee, he saw Simon and his brother Andrew casting a net into the lake, for they were fishermen. [17]"Come, follow me," Jesus said, "and I will send you out to fish for people." [18]At once they left their nets and followed him.

[19]When he had gone a little farther, he saw James son of Zebedee and his brother John in a boat, preparing their nets. [20]Without delay he called them, and they left their father Zebedee in the boat with the hired men and followed him.

Jesus Drives Out an Impure Spirit

[21]They went to Capernaum, and when the Sabbath came, Jesus went into the synagogue and began to teach. [22]The people were amazed at his teaching, because he taught them as one who had authority, not as the teachers of the law. [23]Just then a man in their synagogue who was possessed by an impure spirit cried out, [24]"What do you want with us, Jesus of Nazareth? Have you come to destroy us? I know who you are — the Holy One of God!"

[25]"Be quiet!" said Jesus sternly. "Come out of him!" [26]The impure spirit shook the man violently and came out of him with a shriek.

[27]The people were all so amazed that they asked each other, "What is this? A new teaching — and with authority! He even gives orders to impure spirits and they obey him." [28]News about him spread quickly over the whole region of Galilee.

Jesus Heals Many

[29]As soon as they left the synagogue, they went with James and John to the home of Simon and Andrew. [30]Simon's mother-in-law was in bed with a fever, and they immediately told Jesus about her. [31]So he went to her, took her hand and helped her up. The fever left her and she began to wait on them.

[32]That evening after sunset the people brought to Jesus all the sick and demon-possessed. [33]The whole town gathered at the door, [34]and Jesus healed many who had various diseases. He also drove out many demons, but he would not let the demons speak because they knew who he was.

Jesus Prays in a Solitary Place

[35]Very early in the morning, while it was still dark, Jesus got up, left the house and went off to a solitary place, where he prayed. [36]Simon and his companions went to look for him, [37]and when they found him, they exclaimed: "Everyone is looking for you!"

[38]Jesus replied, "Let us go somewhere else — to the nearby villages — so I can preach there also. That is why I have come." [39]So he traveled throughout Galilee, preaching in their synagogues and driving out demons.

Jesus Heals a Man With Leprosy

[40]A man with leprosy[g] came to him and begged him on his knees, "If you are willing, you can make me clean."

[41]Jesus was indignant.[h] He reached out his hand and touched the man. "I am willing," he said. "Be clean!" [42]Immediately the leprosy left him and he was cleansed.

---

[a] 1 Or Jesus Christ. Messiah (Hebrew) and Christ (Greek) both mean Anointed One.   [b] 1 Some manuscripts do not have the Son of God.   [c] 2 Mal. 3:1   [d] 3 Isaiah 40:3   [e] 8 Or in
[f] 13 The Greek for tempted can also mean tested.   [g] 40 The Greek word traditionally translated leprosy was used for various diseases affecting the skin.   [h] 41 Many manuscripts Jesus was filled with compassion

[43]Jesus sent him away at once with a strong warning: [44]"See that you don't tell this to anyone. But go, show yourself to the priest and offer the sacrifices that Moses commanded for your cleansing, as a testimony to them." [45]Instead he went out and began to talk freely, spreading the news. As a result, Jesus could no longer enter a town openly but stayed outside in lonely places. Yet the people still came to him from everywhere.

Jesus Forgives and Heals a Paralyzed Man

2 A few days later, when Jesus again entered Capernaum, the people heard that he had come home. [2]They gathered in such large numbers that there was no room left, not even outside the door, and he preached the word to them. [3]Some men came, bringing to him a paralyzed man, carried by four of them. [4]Since they could not get him to Jesus because of the crowd, they made an opening in the roof above Jesus by digging through it and then lowered the mat the man was lying on. [5]When Jesus saw their faith, he said to the paralyzed man, "Son, your sins are forgiven."

[6]Now some teachers of the law were sitting there, thinking to themselves, [7]"Why does this fellow talk like that? He's blaspheming! Who can forgive sins but God alone?"

[8]Immediately Jesus knew in his spirit that this was what they were thinking in their hearts, and he said to them, "Why are you thinking these things? [9]Which is easier: to say to this paralyzed man, 'Your sins are forgiven,' or to say, 'Get up, take your mat and walk'? [10]But I want you to know that the Son of Man has authority on earth to forgive sins." So he said to the man, [11]"I tell you, get up, take your mat and go home." [12]He got up, took his mat and walked out in full view of them all. This amazed everyone and they praised God, saying, "We have never seen anything like this!"

Jesus Calls Levi and Eats With Sinners

[13]Once again Jesus went out beside the lake. A large crowd came to him, and he began to teach them. [14]As he walked along, he saw Levi son of Alphaeus sitting at the tax collector's booth. "Follow me," Jesus told him, and Levi got up and followed him.

[15]While Jesus was having dinner at Levi's house, many tax collectors and sinners were eating with him and his disciples, for there were many who followed him. [16]When the teachers of the law who were Pharisees saw him eating with the sinners and tax collectors, they asked his disciples: "Why does he eat with tax collectors and sinners?"

[17]On hearing this, Jesus said to them, "It is not the healthy who need a doctor, but the sick. I have not come to call the righteous, but sinners."

Jesus Questioned About Fasting

[18]Now John's disciples and the Pharisees were fasting. Some people came and asked Jesus, "How is it that John's disciples and the disciples of the Pharisees are fasting, but yours are not?"

[19]Jesus answered, "How can the guests of the bridegroom fast while he is with them? They cannot, so long as they have him with them. [20]But the time will come when the bridegroom will be taken from them, and on that day they will fast.

[21]"No one sews a patch of unshrunk cloth on an old garment. Otherwise, the new piece will pull away from the old, making the tear worse. [22]And no one pours new wine into old wineskins. Otherwise, the wine will burst the skins, and both the wine and the wineskins will be ruined. No, they pour new wine into new wineskins."

Jesus Is Lord of the Sabbath

[23]One Sabbath Jesus was going through the grainfields, and as his disciples walked along, they began to pick some heads of grain. [24]The Pharisees said to him, "Look, why are they doing what is unlawful on the Sabbath?"

[25]He answered, "Have you never read what David did when he and his companions were hungry and in need? [26]In the days of Abiathar the high priest, he entered the house of God and ate the consecrated bread, which is lawful only for priests to eat. And he also gave some to his companions."

[27]Then he said to them, "The Sabbath was made for man, not man for the Sabbath. [28]So the Son of Man is Lord even of the Sabbath."

Jesus Heals on the Sabbath

3 Another time Jesus went into the synagogue, and a man with a shriveled hand was there. [2]Some of them were looking for a reason to accuse Jesus, so they watched him closely to see if he would heal him on the Sabbath. [3]Jesus said to the man with the shriveled hand, "Stand up in front of everyone."

[4]Then Jesus asked them, "Which is lawful on the Sabbath: to do good or to do evil, to save life or to kill?" But they remained silent.

[5]He looked around at them in anger and, deeply distressed at their stubborn hearts, said to the man, "Stretch out your hand." He stretched it out, and his hand was completely restored. [6]Then the Pharisees went out and began to plot with the Herodians how they might kill Jesus.

Crowds Follow Jesus

[7]Jesus withdrew with his disciples to the lake, and a large crowd from Galilee followed. [8]When they heard about all he was doing, many people came to him from Judea, Jerusalem, Idumea, and the regions across the Jordan and around Tyre and Sidon. [9]Because of the crowd he told his disciples to have a small boat ready for him, to keep the people from crowding him. [10]For he had healed many, so that those with diseases were pushing forward to touch him. [11]Whenever the impure spirits saw

him, they fell down before him and cried out, "You are the Son of God." [12]But he gave them strict orders not to tell others about him.

Jesus Appoints the Twelve

[13]Jesus went up on a mountainside and called to him those he wanted, and they came to him. [14]He appointed twelve[a] that they might be with him and that he might send them out to preach [15]and to have authority to drive out demons. [16]These are the twelve he appointed: Simon (to whom he gave the name Peter), [17]James son of Zebedee and his brother John (to them he gave the name Boanerges, which means "sons of thunder"), [18]Andrew, Philip, Bartholomew, Matthew, Thomas, James son of Alphaeus, Thaddaeus, Simon the Zealot [19]and Judas Iscariot, who betrayed him.

Jesus Accused by His Family and by Teachers of the Law

[20]Then Jesus entered a house, and again a crowd gathered, so that he and his disciples were not even able to eat. [21]When his family[b] heard about this, they went to take charge of him, for they said, "He is out of his mind."

[22]And the teachers of the law who came down from Jerusalem said, "He is possessed by Beelzebul! By the prince of demons he is driving out demons."

[23]So Jesus called them over to him and began to speak to them in parables: "How can Satan drive out Satan? [24]If a kingdom is divided against itself, that kingdom cannot stand. [25]If a house is divided against itself, that house cannot stand. [26]And if Satan opposes himself and is divided, he cannot stand; his end has come. [27]In fact, no one can enter a strong man's house without first tying him up. Then he can plunder the strong man's house. [28]Truly I tell you, people can be forgiven all their sins and every slander they utter, [29]but whoever blasphemes against the Holy Spirit will never be forgiven; they are guilty of an eternal sin."

[30]He said this because they were saying, "He has an impure spirit."

[31]Then Jesus' mother and brothers arrived. Standing outside, they sent someone in to call him. [32]A crowd was sitting around him, and they told him, "Your mother and brothers are outside looking for you."

[33]"Who are my mother and my brothers?" he asked.

[34]Then he looked at those seated in a circle around him and said, "Here are my mother and my brothers! [35]Whoever does God's will is my brother and sister and mother."

The Parable of the Sower

4 Again Jesus began to teach by the lake. The crowd that gathered around him was so large that he got into a boat and sat in it out on the lake, while all the people were along the shore at the water's edge. [2]He taught them many things by parables, and in his teaching said:

[3]"Listen! A farmer went out to sow his seed. [4]As he was scattering the seed, some fell along the path, and the birds came and ate it up. [5]Some fell on rocky places, where it did not have much soil. It sprang up quickly, because the soil was shallow. [6]But when the sun came up, the plants were scorched, and they withered because they had no root. [7]Other seed fell among thorns, which grew up and choked the plants, so that they did not bear grain. [8]Still other seed fell on good soil. It came up, grew and produced a crop, some multiplying thirty, some sixty, some a hundred times."

[9]Then Jesus said, "Whoever has ears to hear, let them hear."

[10]When he was alone, the Twelve and the others around him asked him about the parables. [11]He told them, "The secret of the kingdom of God has been given to you. But to those on the outside everything is said in parables [12]so that,

> "'they may be ever seeing but never perceiving,
>   and ever hearing but never understanding;
> otherwise they might turn and be forgiven!'[c]"

[13]Then Jesus said to them, "Don't you understand this parable? How then will you understand any parable? [14]The farmer sows the word. [15]Some people are like seed along the path, where the word is sown. As soon as they hear it, Satan comes and takes away the word that was sown in them. [16]Others, like seed sown on rocky places, hear the word and at once receive it with joy. [17]But since they have no root, they last only a short time. When trouble or persecution comes because of the word, they quickly fall away. [18]Still others, like seed sown among thorns, hear the word; [19]but the worries of this life, the deceitfulness of wealth and the desires for other things come in and choke the word, making it unfruitful. [20]Others, like seed sown on good soil, hear the word, accept it, and produce a crop—some thirty, some sixty, some a hundred times what was sown."

A Lamp on a Stand

[21]He said to them, "Do you bring in a lamp to put it under a bowl or a bed? Instead, don't you put it on its stand? [22]For whatever is hidden is meant to be disclosed, and whatever is concealed is meant to be brought out into the open. [23]If anyone has ears to hear, let them hear."

[24]"Consider carefully what you hear," he continued. "With the measure you use, it will be measured to you—and even more. [25]Whoever has will be given more; whoever does not have, even what they have will be taken from them."

The Parable of the Growing Seed

[26]He also said, "This is what the kingdom of God is like. A man scatters seed on the ground. [27]Night and day, whether he sleeps or gets up,

---

[a] 14 Some manuscripts *twelve—designating them apostles—*   [b] 21 Or *his associates*   [c] 12 Isaiah 6:9,10

the seed sprouts and grows, though he does not know how. ²⁸All by itself the soil produces grain — first the stalk, then the head, then the full kernel in the head. ²⁹As soon as the grain is ripe, he puts the sickle to it, because the harvest has come."

The Parable of the Mustard Seed

³⁰Again he said, "What shall we say the kingdom of God is like, or what parable shall we use to describe it? ³¹It is like a mustard seed, which is the smallest of all seeds on earth. ³²Yet when planted, it grows and becomes the largest of all garden plants, with such big branches that the birds can perch in its shade."

³³With many similar parables Jesus spoke the word to them, as much as they could understand. ³⁴He did not say anything to them without using a parable. But when he was alone with his own disciples, he explained everything.

Jesus Calms the Storm

³⁵That day when evening came, he said to his disciples, "Let us go over to the other side." ³⁶Leaving the crowd behind, they took him along, just as he was, in the boat. There were also other boats with him. ³⁷A furious squall came up, and the waves broke over the boat, so that it was nearly swamped. ³⁸Jesus was in the stern, sleeping on a cushion. The disciples woke him and said to him, "Teacher, don't you care if we drown?"

³⁹He got up, rebuked the wind and said to the waves, "Quiet! Be still!" Then the wind died down and it was completely calm.

⁴⁰He said to his disciples, "Why are you so afraid? Do you still have no faith?"

⁴¹They were terrified and asked each other, "Who is this? Even the wind and the waves obey him!"

Jesus Restores a Demon-Possessed Man

5 They went across the lake to the region of the Gerasenes.ᵃ ²When Jesus got out of the boat, a man with an impure spirit came from the tombs to meet him. ³This man lived in the tombs, and no one could bind him anymore, not even with a chain. ⁴For he had often been chained hand and foot, but he tore the chains apart and broke the irons on his feet. No one was strong enough to subdue him. ⁵Night and day among the tombs and in the hills he would cry out and cut himself with stones.

⁶When he saw Jesus from a distance, he ran and fell on his knees in front of him. ⁷He shouted at the top of his voice, "What do you want with me, Jesus, Son of the Most High God? In God's name don't torture me!" ⁸For Jesus had said to him, "Come out of this man, you impure spirit!"

⁹Then Jesus asked him, "What is your name?"

"My name is Legion," he replied, "for we are many." ¹⁰And he begged Jesus again and again not to send them out of the area.

¹¹A large herd of pigs was feeding on the nearby hillside. ¹²The demons begged Jesus, "Send us among the pigs; allow us to go into them." ¹³He gave them permission, and the impure spirits came out and went into the pigs. The herd, about two thousand in number, rushed down the steep bank into the lake and were drowned.

¹⁴Those tending the pigs ran off and reported this in the town and countryside, and the people went out to see what had happened. ¹⁵When they came to Jesus, they saw the man who had been possessed by the legion of demons, sitting there, dressed and in his right mind; and they were afraid. ¹⁶Those who had seen it told the people what had happened to the demon-possessed man — and told about the pigs as well. ¹⁷Then the people began to plead with Jesus to leave their region.

¹⁸As Jesus was getting into the boat, the man who had been demon-possessed begged to go with him. ¹⁹Jesus did not let him, but said, "Go home to your own people and tell them how much the Lord has done for you, and how he has had mercy on you." ²⁰So the man went away and began to tell in the Decapolisᵇ how much Jesus had done for him. And all the people were amazed.

Jesus Raises a Dead Girl and Heals a Sick Woman

²¹When Jesus had again crossed over by boat to the other side of the lake, a large crowd gathered around him while he was by the lake. ²²Then one of the synagogue leaders, named Jairus, came, and when he saw Jesus, he fell at his feet. ²³He pleaded earnestly with him, "My little daughter is dying. Please come and put your hands on her so that she will be healed and live." ²⁴So Jesus went with him.

A large crowd followed and pressed around him. ²⁵And a woman was there who had been subject to bleeding for twelve years. ²⁶She had suffered a great deal under the care of many doctors and had spent all she had, yet instead of getting better she grew worse. ²⁷When she heard about Jesus, she came up behind him in the crowd and touched his cloak, ²⁸because she thought, "If I just touch his clothes, I will be healed." ²⁹Immediately her bleeding stopped and she felt in her body that she was freed from her suffering.

³⁰At once Jesus realized that power had gone out from him. He turned around in the crowd and asked, "Who touched my clothes?"

³¹"You see the people crowding against you," his disciples answered, "and yet you can ask, 'Who touched me?' "

³²But Jesus kept looking around to see who had done it. ³³Then the woman, knowing what had happened to her, came and fell at his feet and, trembling with fear, told him the whole truth. ³⁴He said to her,

---

ᵃ *1* Some manuscripts *Gadarenes*; other manuscripts *Gergesenes*   ᵇ *20* That is, the Ten Cities

"Daughter, your faith has healed you. Go in peace and be freed from your suffering."

³⁵While Jesus was still speaking, some people came from the house of Jairus, the synagogue leader. "Your daughter is dead," they said. "Why bother the teacher anymore?"

³⁶Overhearing[a] what they said, Jesus told him, "Don't be afraid; just believe."

³⁷He did not let anyone follow him except Peter, James and John the brother of James. ³⁸When they came to the home of the synagogue leader, Jesus saw a commotion, with people crying and wailing loudly. ³⁹He went in and said to them, "Why all this commotion and wailing? The child is not dead but asleep." ⁴⁰But they laughed at him.

After he put them all out, he took the child's father and mother and the disciples who were with him, and went in where the child was. ⁴¹He took her by the hand and said to her, *Talitha koum!*" (which means "Little girl, I say to you, get up!"). ⁴²Immediately the girl stood up and began to walk around (she was twelve years old). At this they were completely astonished. ⁴³He gave strict orders not to let anyone know about this, and told them to give her something to eat.

A Prophet Without Honor

6 Jesus left there and went to his hometown, accompanied by his disciples. ²When the Sabbath came, he began to teach in the synagogue, and many who heard him were amazed.

"Where did this man get these things?" they asked. "What's this wisdom that has been given him? What are these remarkable miracles he is performing? ³Isn't this the carpenter? Isn't this Mary's son and the brother of James, Joseph,[b] Judas and Simon? Aren't his sisters here with us?" And they took offense at him.

⁴Jesus said to them, "A prophet is not without honor except in his own town, among his relatives and in his own home." ⁵He could not do any miracles there, except lay his hands on a few sick people and heal them. ⁶He was amazed at their lack of faith.

Jesus Sends Out the Twelve

Then Jesus went around teaching from village to village. ⁷Calling the Twelve to him, he began to send them out two by two and gave them authority over impure spirits.

⁸These were his instructions: "Take nothing for the journey except a staff—no bread, no bag, no money in your belts. ⁹Wear sandals but not an extra shirt. ¹⁰Whenever you enter a house, stay there until you leave that town. ¹¹And if any place will not welcome you or listen to you, leave that place and shake the dust off your feet as a testimony against them."

¹²They went out and preached that people should repent. ¹³They drove out many demons and anointed many sick people with oil and healed them.

John the Baptist Beheaded

¹⁴King Herod heard about this, for Jesus' name had become well known. Some were saying,[c] "John the Baptist has been raised from the dead, and that is why miraculous powers are at work in him."

¹⁵Others said, "He is Elijah."

And still others claimed, "He is a prophet, like one of the prophets of long ago."

¹⁶But when Herod heard this, he said, "John, whom I beheaded, has been raised from the dead!"

¹⁷For Herod himself had given orders to have John arrested, and he had him bound and put in prison. He did this because of Herodias, his brother Philip's wife, whom he had married. ¹⁸For John had been saying to Herod, "It is not lawful for you to have your brother's wife." ¹⁹So Herodias nursed a grudge against John and wanted to kill him. But she was not able to, ²⁰because Herod feared John and protected him, knowing him to be a righteous and holy man. When Herod heard John, he was greatly puzzled[d]; yet he liked to listen to him.

²¹Finally the opportune time came. On his birthday Herod gave a banquet for his high officials and military commanders and the leading men of Galilee. ²²When the daughter of[e] Herodias came in and danced, she pleased Herod and his dinner guests.

The king said to the girl, "Ask me for anything you want, and I'll give it to you." ²³And he promised her with an oath, "Whatever you ask I will give you, up to half my kingdom."

²⁴She went out and said to her mother, "What shall I ask for?"

"The head of John the Baptist," she answered.

²⁵At once the girl hurried in to the king with the request: "I want you to give me right now the head of John the Baptist on a platter."

²⁶The king was greatly distressed, but because of his oaths and his dinner guests, he did not want to refuse her. ²⁷So he immediately sent an executioner with orders to bring John's head. The man went, beheaded John in the prison, ²⁸and brought back his head on a platter. He presented it to the girl, and she gave it to her mother. ²⁹On hearing of this, John's disciples came and took his body and laid it in a tomb.

Jesus Feeds the Five Thousand

³⁰The apostles gathered around Jesus and reported to him all they had done and taught. ³¹Then, because so many people were coming and going that they did not even have a chance to eat, he said to them, "Come with me by yourselves to a quiet place and get some rest."

---

a 36 Or *Ignoring*   *b 3* Greek *Joses*, a variant of *Joseph*   *c 14* Some early manuscripts *He was saying*   *d 20* Some early manuscripts *he did many things*   *e 22* Some early manuscripts *When his daughter*

³²So they went away by themselves in a boat to a solitary place. ³³But many who saw them leaving recognized them and ran on foot from all the towns and got there ahead of them. ³⁴When Jesus landed and saw a large crowd, he had compassion on them, because they were like sheep without a shepherd. So he began teaching them many things.

³⁵By this time it was late in the day, so his disciples came to him. "This is a remote place," they said, "and it's already very late. ³⁶Send the people away so that they can go to the surrounding countryside and villages and buy themselves something to eat."

³⁷But he answered, "You give them something to eat."

They said to him, "That would take more than half a year's wages*ᵃ! Are we to go and spend that much on bread and give it to them to eat?"

³⁸"How many loaves do you have?" he asked. "Go and see."

When they found out, they said, "Five — and two fish."

³⁹Then Jesus directed them to have all the people sit down in groups on the green grass. ⁴⁰So they sat down in groups of hundreds and fifties. ⁴¹Taking the five loaves and the two fish and looking up to heaven, he gave thanks and broke the loaves. Then he gave them to his disciples to distribute to the people. He also divided the two fish among them all. ⁴²They all ate and were satisfied, ⁴³and the disciples picked up twelve basketfuls of broken pieces of bread and fish. ⁴⁴The number of the men who had eaten was five thousand.

Jesus Walks on the Water

⁴⁵Immediately Jesus made his disciples get into the boat and go on ahead of him to Bethsaida, while he dismissed the crowd. ⁴⁶After leaving them, he went up on a mountainside to pray.

⁴⁷Later that night, the boat was in the middle of the lake, and he was alone on land. ⁴⁸He saw the disciples straining at the oars, because the wind was against them. Shortly before dawn he went out to them, walking on the lake. He was about to pass by them, ⁴⁹but when they saw him walking on the lake, they thought he was a ghost. They cried out, ⁵⁰because they all saw him and were terrified.

Immediately he spoke to them and said, "Take courage! It is I. Don't be afraid." ⁵¹Then he climbed into the boat with them, and the wind died down. They were completely amazed, ⁵²for they had not understood about the loaves; their hearts were hardened.

⁵³When they had crossed over, they landed at Gennesaret and anchored there. ⁵⁴As soon as they got out of the boat, people recognized Jesus. ⁵⁵They ran throughout that whole region and carried the sick on mats to wherever they heard he was. ⁵⁶And wherever he went — into villages, towns or countryside — they placed the sick in the marketplaces. They begged him to let them touch even the edge of his cloak, and all who touched it were healed.

That Which Defiles

7 The Pharisees and some of the teachers of the law who had come from Jerusalem gathered around Jesus ²and saw some of his disciples eating food with hands that were defiled, that is, unwashed. ³(The Pharisees and all the Jews do not eat unless they give their hands a ceremonial washing, holding to the tradition of the elders. ⁴When they come from the marketplace they do not eat unless they wash. And they observe many other traditions, such as the washing of cups, pitchers and kettles.ᵇ)

⁵So the Pharisees and teachers of the law asked Jesus, "Why don't your disciples live according to the tradition of the elders instead of eating their food with defiled hands?"

⁶He replied, "Isaiah was right when he prophesied about you hypocrites; as it is written:

"'These people honor me with their lips,
    but their hearts are far from me.
⁷ They worship me in vain;
    their teachings are merely human rules.'ᶜ

⁸You have let go of the commands of God and are holding on to human traditions."

⁹And he continued, "You have a fine way of setting aside the commands of God in order to observeᵈ your own traditions! ¹⁰For Moses said, 'Honor your father and mother,'ᵉ and, 'Anyone who curses their father or mother is to be put to death.'ᶠ ¹¹But you say that if anyone declares that what might have been used to help their father or mother is Corban (that is, devoted to God) — ¹²then you no longer let them do anything for their father or mother. ¹³Thus you nullify the word of God by your tradition that you have handed down. And you do many things like that."

¹⁴Again Jesus called the crowd to him and said, "Listen to me, everyone, and understand this. ¹⁵Nothing outside a person can defile them by going into them. Rather, it is what comes out of a person that defiles them." [16]ᵍ

¹⁷After he had left the crowd and entered the house, his disciples asked him about this parable. ¹⁸"Are you so dull?" he asked. "Don't you see that nothing that enters a person from the outside can defile them? ¹⁹For it doesn't go into their heart but into their stomach, and then out of the body." (In saying this, Jesus declared all foods clean.)

²⁰He went on: "What comes out of a person is what defiles them. ²¹For it is from within, out of a person's heart, that evil thoughts come — sexual immorality, theft, murder, ²²adultery, greed, malice, deceit, lewdness, envy, slander, arrogance and folly. ²³All these evils come from inside and defile a person."

ᵃ 37 Greek *take two hundred denarii*   ᵇ 4 Some early manuscripts *pitchers, kettles and dining couches*   ᶜ 6,7 Isaiah 29:13   ᵈ 9 Some manuscripts *set up*   ᵉ 10 Exodus 20:12; Deut. 5:16   ᶠ 10 Exodus 21:17; Lev. 20:9   ᵍ 16 Some manuscripts include here the words of 4:23.

Jesus Honors a Syrophoenician Woman's Faith

[24]Jesus left that place and went to the vicinity of Tyre.[a] He entered a house and did not want anyone to know it; yet he could not keep his presence secret. [25]In fact, as soon as she heard about him, a woman whose little daughter was possessed by an impure spirit came and fell at his feet. [26]The woman was a Greek, born in Syrian Phoenicia. She begged Jesus to drive the demon out of her daughter.

[27]"First let the children eat all they want," he told her, "for it is not right to take the children's bread and toss it to the dogs."

[28]"Lord," she replied, "even the dogs under the table eat the children's crumbs."

[29]Then he told her, "For such a reply, you may go; the demon has left your daughter."

[30]She went home and found her child lying on the bed, and the demon gone.

Jesus Heals a Deaf and Mute Man

[31]Then Jesus left the vicinity of Tyre and went through Sidon, down to the Sea of Galilee and into the region of the Decapolis.[b] [32]There some people brought to him a man who was deaf and could hardly talk, and they begged Jesus to place his hand on him.

[33]After he took him aside, away from the crowd, Jesus put his fingers into the man's ears. Then he spit and touched the man's tongue. [34]He looked up to heaven and with a deep sigh said to him, *"Ephphatha!"* (which means "Be opened!"). [35]At this, the man's ears were opened, his tongue was loosened and he began to speak plainly.

[36]Jesus commanded them not to tell anyone. But the more he did so, the more they kept talking about it. [37]People were overwhelmed with amazement. "He has done everything well," they said. "He even makes the deaf hear and the mute speak."

Jesus Feeds the Four Thousand

8 During those days another large crowd gathered. Since they had nothing to eat, Jesus called his disciples to him and said, [2]"I have compassion for these people; they have already been with me three days and have nothing to eat. [3]If I send them home hungry, they will collapse on the way, because some of them have come a long distance."

[4]His disciples answered, "But where in this remote place can anyone get enough bread to feed them?"

[5]"How many loaves do you have?" Jesus asked.

"Seven," they replied.

[6]He told the crowd to sit down on the ground. When he had taken the seven loaves and given thanks, he broke them and gave them to his disciples to distribute to the people, and they did so. [7]They had a few small fish as well; he gave thanks for them also and told the disciples to distribute them. [8]The people ate and were satisfied. Afterward the disciples picked up seven basketfuls of broken pieces that were left over. [9]About four thousand were present. After he had sent them away, [10]he got into the boat with his disciples and went to the region of Dalmanutha.

[11]The Pharisees came and began to question Jesus. To test him, they asked him for a sign from heaven. [12]He sighed deeply and said, "Why does this generation ask for a sign? Truly I tell you, no sign will be given to it." [13]Then he left them, got back into the boat and crossed to the other side.

The Yeast of the Pharisees and Herod

[14]The disciples had forgotten to bring bread, except for one loaf they had with them in the boat. [15]"Be careful," Jesus warned them. "Watch out for the yeast of the Pharisees and that of Herod."

[16]They discussed this with one another and said, "It is because we have no bread."

[17]Aware of their discussion, Jesus asked them: "Why are you talking about having no bread? Do you still not see or understand? Are your hearts hardened? [18]Do you have eyes but fail to see, and ears but fail to hear? And don't you remember? [19]When I broke the five loaves for the five thousand, how many basketfuls of pieces did you pick up?"

"Twelve," they replied.

[20]"And when I broke the seven loaves for the four thousand, how many basketfuls of pieces did you pick up?"

They answered, "Seven."

[21]He said to them, "Do you still not understand?"

Jesus Heals a Blind Man at Bethsaida

[22]They came to Bethsaida, and some people brought a blind man and begged Jesus to touch him. [23]He took the blind man by the hand and led him outside the village. When he had spit on the man's eyes and put his hands on him, Jesus asked, "Do you see anything?"

[24]He looked up and said, "I see people; they look like trees walking around."

[25]Once more Jesus put his hands on the man's eyes. Then his eyes were opened, his sight was restored, and he saw everything clearly. [26]Jesus sent him home, saying, "Don't even go into[c] the village."

Peter Declares That Jesus Is the Messiah

[27]Jesus and his disciples went on to the villages around Caesarea Philippi. On the way he asked them, "Who do people say I am?"

[28]They replied, "Some say John the Baptist; others say Elijah; and still others, one of the prophets."

[29]"But what about you?" he asked. "Who do you say I am?"

Peter answered, "You are the Messiah."

[30]Jesus warned them not to tell anyone about him.

Jesus Predicts His Death

[31]He then began to teach them that the Son of Man must suffer many things and be rejected by the elders, the chief priests and the teachers of the law, and that he must be killed and after three days rise again. [32]He spoke plainly about this, and Peter took him aside and began to rebuke him.

[33]But when Jesus turned and looked at his disciples, he rebuked Peter. "Get behind me, Satan!" he said. "You do not have in mind the concerns of God, but merely human concerns."

The Way of the Cross

[34]Then he called the crowd to him along with his disciples and said: "Whoever wants to be my disciple must deny themselves and take up their cross and follow me. [35]For whoever wants to save their life[a] will lose it, but whoever loses their life for me and for the gospel will save it. [36]What good is it for someone to gain the whole world, yet forfeit their soul? [37]Or what can anyone give in exchange for their soul? [38]If anyone is ashamed of me and my words in this adulterous and sinful generation, the Son of Man will be ashamed of them when he comes in his Father's glory with the holy angels."

9 And he said to them, "Truly I tell you, some who are standing here will not taste death before they see that the kingdom of God has come with power."

The Transfiguration

[2]After six days Jesus took Peter, James and John with him and led them up a high mountain, where they were all alone. There he was transfigured before them. [3]His clothes became dazzling white, whiter than anyone in the world could bleach them. [4]And there appeared before them Elijah and Moses, who were talking with Jesus.

[5]Peter said to Jesus, "Rabbi, it is good for us to be here. Let us put up three shelters — one for you, one for Moses and one for Elijah." [6](He did not know what to say, they were so frightened.)

[7]Then a cloud appeared and covered them, and a voice came from the cloud: "This is my Son, whom I love. Listen to him!"

[8]Suddenly, when they looked around, they no longer saw anyone with them except Jesus.

[9]As they were coming down the mountain, Jesus gave them orders not to tell anyone what they had seen until the Son of Man had risen from the dead. [10]They kept the matter to themselves, discussing what "rising from the dead" meant.

[11]And they asked him, "Why do the teachers of the law say that Elijah must come first?"

[12]Jesus replied, "To be sure, Elijah does come first, and restores all things. Why then is it written that the Son of Man must suffer much and be rejected? [13]But I tell you, Elijah has come, and they have done to him everything they wished, just as it is written about him."

Jesus Heals a Boy Possessed by an Impure Spirit

[14]When they came to the other disciples, they saw a large crowd around them and the teachers of the law arguing with them. [15]As soon as all the people saw Jesus, they were overwhelmed with wonder and ran to greet him.

[16]"What are you arguing with them about?" he asked.

[17]A man in the crowd answered, "Teacher, I brought you my son, who is possessed by a spirit that has robbed him of speech. [18]Whenever it seizes him, it throws him to the ground. He foams at the mouth, gnashes his teeth and becomes rigid. I asked your disciples to drive out the spirit, but they could not."

[19]"You unbelieving generation," Jesus replied, "how long shall I stay with you? How long shall I put up with you? Bring the boy to me."

[20]So they brought him. When the spirit saw Jesus, it immediately threw the boy into a convulsion. He fell to the ground and rolled around, foaming at the mouth.

[21]Jesus asked the boy's father, "How long has he been like this?"

"From childhood," he answered. [22]"It has often thrown him into fire or water to kill him. But if you can do anything, take pity on us and help us."

[23]"'If you can'?" said Jesus. "Everything is possible for one who believes."

[24]Immediately the boy's father exclaimed, "I do believe; help me overcome my unbelief!"

[25]When Jesus saw that a crowd was running to the scene, he rebuked the impure spirit. "You deaf and mute spirit," he said, "I command you, come out of him and never enter him again."

[26]The spirit shrieked, convulsed him violently and came out. The boy looked so much like a corpse that many said, "He's dead." [27]But Jesus took him by the hand and lifted him to his feet, and he stood up.

[28]After Jesus had gone indoors, his disciples asked him privately, "Why couldn't we drive it out?"

[29]He replied, "This kind can come out only by prayer.[b]"

---

[a] 35 The Greek word means either *life* or *soul*; also in verses 36 and 37.   [b] 29 Some manuscripts *prayer and fasting*

Jesus Predicts His Death a Second Time

[30]They left that place and passed through Galilee. Jesus did not want anyone to know where they were, [31]because he was teaching his disciples. He said to them, "The Son of Man is going to be delivered into the hands of men. They will kill him, and after three days he will rise." [32]But they did not understand what he meant and were afraid to ask him about it.

[33]They came to Capernaum. When he was in the house, he asked them, "What were you arguing about on the road?" [34]But they kept quiet because on the way they had argued about who was the greatest.

[35]Sitting down, Jesus called the Twelve and said, "Anyone who wants to be first must be the very last, and the servant of all."

[36]He took a little child whom he placed among them. Taking the child in his arms, he said to them, [37]"Whoever welcomes one of these little children in my name welcomes me; and whoever welcomes me does not welcome me but the one who sent me."

Whoever Is Not Against Us Is for Us

[38]"Teacher," said John, "we saw someone driving out demons in your name and we told him to stop, because he was not one of us."

[39]"Do not stop him," Jesus said. "For no one who does a miracle in my name can in the next moment say anything bad about me, [40]for whoever is not against us is for us. [41]Truly I tell you, anyone who gives you a cup of water in my name because you belong to the Messiah will certainly not lose their reward.

Causing to Stumble

[42]"If anyone causes one of these little ones — those who believe in me — to stumble, it would be better for them if a large millstone were hung around their neck and they were thrown into the sea. [43]If your hand causes you to stumble, cut it off. It is better for you to enter life maimed than with two hands to go into hell, where the fire never goes out. [44]*a* [45]And if your foot causes you to stumble, cut it off. It is better for you to enter life crippled than to have two feet and be thrown into hell. [46]*a* [47]And if your eye causes you to stumble, pluck it out. It is better for you to enter the kingdom of God with one eye than to have two eyes and be thrown into hell, [48]where

" 'the worms that eat them do not die,
    and the fire is not quenched.'*b*

[49]Everyone will be salted with fire.

[50]"Salt is good, but if it loses its saltiness, how can you make it salty again? Have salt among yourselves, and be at peace with each other."

Divorce

10 Jesus then left that place and went into the region of Judea and across the Jordan. Again crowds of people came to him, and as was his custom, he taught them.

[2]Some Pharisees came and tested him by asking, "Is it lawful for a man to divorce his wife?"

[3]"What did Moses command you?" he replied.

[4]They said, "Moses permitted a man to write a certificate of divorce and send her away."

[5]"It was because your hearts were hard that Moses wrote you this law," Jesus replied. [6]"But at the beginning of creation God 'made them male and female.'*c* [7]'For this reason a man will leave his father and mother and be united to his wife,*d* [8]and the two will become one flesh.'*e* So they are no longer two, but one flesh. [9]Therefore what God has joined together, let no one separate."

[10]When they were in the house again, the disciples asked Jesus about this. [11]He answered, "Anyone who divorces his wife and marries another woman commits adultery against her. [12]And if she divorces her husband and marries another man, she commits adultery."

The Little Children and Jesus

[13]People were bringing little children to Jesus for him to place his hands on them, but the disciples rebuked them. [14]When Jesus saw this, he was indignant. He said to them, "Let the little children come to me, and do not hinder them, for the kingdom of God belongs to such as these. [15]Truly I tell you, anyone who will not receive the kingdom of God like a little child will never enter it." [16]And he took the children in his arms, placed his hands on them and blessed them.

The Rich and the Kingdom of God

[17]As Jesus started on his way, a man ran up to him and fell on his knees before him. "Good teacher," he asked, "what must I do to inherit eternal life?"

[18]"Why do you call me good?" Jesus answered. "No one is good — except God alone. [19]You know the commandments: 'You shall not murder, you shall not commit adultery, you shall not steal, you shall not give false testimony, you shall not defraud, honor your father and mother.'*f*"

[20]"Teacher," he declared, "all these I have kept since I was a boy."

[21]Jesus looked at him and loved him. "One thing you lack," he said. "Go, sell everything you have and give to the poor, and you will have treasure in heaven. Then come, follow me."

[22]At this the man's face fell. He went away sad, because he had great wealth.

---

a 44,46 Some manuscripts include here the words of verse 48.   *b 48* Isaiah 66:24   *c 6* Gen. 1:27   *d 7* Some early manuscripts do not have *and be united to his wife.*   *e 8* Gen. 2:24
f 19 Exodus 20:12-16; Deut. 5:16-20

[23]Jesus looked around and said to his disciples, "How hard it is for the rich to enter the kingdom of God!"

[24]The disciples were amazed at his words. But Jesus said again, "Children, how hard it is[a] to enter the kingdom of God! [25]It is easier for a camel to go through the eye of a needle than for someone who is rich to enter the kingdom of God."

[26]The disciples were even more amazed, and said to each other, "Who then can be saved?"

[27]Jesus looked at them and said, "With man this is impossible, but not with God; all things are possible with God."

[28]Then Peter spoke up, "We have left everything to follow you!"

[29]"Truly I tell you," Jesus replied, "no one who has left home or brothers or sisters or mother or father or children or fields for me and the gospel [30]will fail to receive a hundred times as much in this present age: homes, brothers, sisters, mothers, children and fields — along with persecutions — and in the age to come eternal life. [31]But many who are first will be last, and the last first."

Jesus Predicts His Death a Third Time

[32]They were on their way up to Jerusalem, with Jesus leading the way, and the disciples were astonished, while those who followed were afraid. Again he took the Twelve aside and told them what was going to happen to him. [33]"We are going up to Jerusalem," he said, "and the Son of Man will be delivered over to the chief priests and the teachers of the law. They will condemn him to death and will hand him over to the Gentiles, [34]who will mock him and spit on him, flog him and kill him. Three days later he will rise."

The Request of James and John

[35]Then James and John, the sons of Zebedee, came to him. "Teacher," they said, "we want you to do for us whatever we ask."

[36]"What do you want me to do for you?" he asked.

[37]They replied, "Let one of us sit at your right and the other at your left in your glory."

[38]"You don't know what you are asking," Jesus said. "Can you drink the cup I drink or be baptized with the baptism I am baptized with?"

[39]"We can," they answered.

Jesus said to them, "You will drink the cup I drink and be baptized with the baptism I am baptized with, [40]but to sit at my right or left is not for me to grant. These places belong to those for whom they have been prepared."

[41]When the ten heard about this, they became indignant with James and John. [42]Jesus called them together and said, "You know that those who are regarded as rulers of the Gentiles lord it over them, and their high officials exercise authority over them. [43]Not so with you. Instead, whoever wants to become great among you must be your servant, [44]and whoever wants to be first must be slave of all. [45]For even the Son of Man did not come to be served, but to serve, and to give his life as a ransom for many."

Blind Bartimaeus Receives His Sight

[46]Then they came to Jericho. As Jesus and his disciples, together with a large crowd, were leaving the city, a blind man, Bartimaeus (which means "son of Timaeus"), was sitting by the roadside begging. [47]When he heard that it was Jesus of Nazareth, he began to shout, "Jesus, Son of David, have mercy on me!"

[48]Many rebuked him and told him to be quiet, but he shouted all the more, "Son of David, have mercy on me!"

[49]Jesus stopped and said, "Call him."

So they called to the blind man, "Cheer up! On your feet! He's calling you." [50]Throwing his cloak aside, he jumped to his feet and came to Jesus.

[51]"What do you want me to do for you?" Jesus asked him.

The blind man said, "Rabbi, I want to see."

[52]"Go," said Jesus, "your faith has healed you." Immediately he received his sight and followed Jesus along the road.

Jesus Comes to Jerusalem as King

11 As they approached Jerusalem and came to Bethphage and Bethany at the Mount of Olives, Jesus sent two of his disciples, [2]saying to them, "Go to the village ahead of you, and just as you enter it, you will find a colt tied there, which no one has ever ridden. Untie it and bring it here. [3]If anyone asks you, 'Why are you doing this?' say, 'The Lord needs it and will send it back here shortly.'"

[4]They went and found a colt outside in the street, tied at a doorway. As they untied it, [5]some people standing there asked, "What are you doing, untying that colt?" [6]They answered as Jesus had told them to, and the people let them go. [7]When they brought the colt to Jesus and threw their cloaks over it, he sat on it. [8]Many people spread their cloaks on the road, while others spread branches they had cut in the fields. [9]Those who went ahead and those who followed shouted,

"Hosanna![b]"

"Blessed is he who comes in the name of the Lord!"[c]

[10]"Blessed is the coming kingdom of our father David!"

"Hosanna in the highest heaven!"

[11]Jesus entered Jerusalem and went into the temple courts. He looked around at everything, but since it was already late, he went out to Bethany with the Twelve.

---

[a] 24 Some manuscripts *is for those who trust in riches*   [b] 9 A Hebrew expression meaning "Save!" which became an exclamation of praise; also in verse 10   [c] 9 Psalm 118:25,26

Jesus Curses a Fig Tree and Clears the Temple Courts

¹²The next day as they were leaving Bethany, Jesus was hungry. ¹³Seeing in the distance a fig tree in leaf, he went to find out if it had any fruit. When he reached it, he found nothing but leaves, because it was not the season for figs. ¹⁴Then he said to the tree, "May no one ever eat fruit from you again." And his disciples heard him say it.

¹⁵On reaching Jerusalem, Jesus entered the temple courts and began driving out those who were buying and selling there. He overturned the tables of the money changers and the benches of those selling doves, ¹⁶and would not allow anyone to carry merchandise through the temple courts. ¹⁷And as he taught them, he said, "Is it not written: 'My house will be called a house of prayer for all nations'*a*? But you have made it 'a den of robbers.'*b*"

¹⁸The chief priests and the teachers of the law heard this and began looking for a way to kill him, for they feared him, because the whole crowd was amazed at his teaching.

¹⁹When evening came, Jesus and his disciples*c* went out of the city.

²⁰In the morning, as they went along, they saw the fig tree withered from the roots. ²¹Peter remembered and said to Jesus, "Rabbi, look! The fig tree you cursed has withered!"

²²"Have faith in God," Jesus answered. ²³"Truly*d* I tell you, if anyone says to this mountain, 'Go, throw yourself into the sea,' and does not doubt in their heart but believes that what they say will happen, it will be done for them. ²⁴Therefore I tell you, whatever you ask for in prayer, believe that you have received it, and it will be yours. ²⁵And when you stand praying, if you hold anything against anyone, forgive them, so that your Father in heaven may forgive you your sins." [26]*e*

The Authority of Jesus Questioned

²⁷They arrived again in Jerusalem, and while Jesus was walking in the temple courts, the chief priests, the teachers of the law and the elders came to him. ²⁸"By what authority are you doing these things?" they asked. "And who gave you authority to do this?"

²⁹Jesus replied, "I will ask you one question. Answer me, and I will tell you by what authority I am doing these things. ³⁰John's baptism — was it from heaven, or of human origin? Tell me!"

³¹They discussed it among themselves and said, "If we say, 'From heaven,' he will ask, 'Then why didn't you believe him?' ³²But if we say, 'Of human origin' . . ." (They feared the people, for everyone held that John really was a prophet.)

³³So they answered Jesus, "We don't know."

Jesus said, "Neither will I tell you by what authority I am doing these things."

The Parable of the Tenants

12 Jesus then began to speak to them in parables: "A man planted a vineyard. He put a wall around it, dug a pit for the winepress and built a watchtower. Then he rented the vineyard to some farmers and moved to another place. ²At harvest time he sent a servant to the tenants to collect from them some of the fruit of the vineyard. ³But they seized him, beat him and sent him away empty-handed. ⁴Then he sent another servant to them; they struck this man on the head and treated him shamefully. ⁵He sent still another, and that one they killed. He sent many others; some of them they beat, others they killed.

⁶"He had one left to send, a son, whom he loved. He sent him last of all, saying, 'They will respect my son.'

⁷"But the tenants said to one another, 'This is the heir. Come, let's kill him, and the inheritance will be ours.' ⁸So they took him and killed him, and threw him out of the vineyard.

⁹"What then will the owner of the vineyard do? He will come and kill those tenants and give the vineyard to others. ¹⁰Haven't you read this passage of Scripture:

"'The stone the builders rejected
    has become the cornerstone;
¹¹the Lord has done this,
    and it is marvelous in our eyes'*f*?"

¹²Then the chief priests, the teachers of the law and the elders looked for a way to arrest him because they knew he had spoken the parable against them. But they were afraid of the crowd; so they left him and went away.

Paying the Imperial Tax to Caesar

¹³Later they sent some of the Pharisees and Herodians to Jesus to catch him in his words. ¹⁴They came to him and said, "Teacher, we know that you are a man of integrity. You aren't swayed by others, because you pay no attention to who they are; but you teach the way of God in accordance with the truth. Is it right to pay the imperial tax*g* to Caesar or not? ¹⁵Should we pay or shouldn't we?"

But Jesus knew their hypocrisy. "Why are you trying to trap me?" he asked. "Bring me a denarius and let me look at it." ¹⁶They brought the coin, and he asked them, "Whose image is this? And whose inscription?"

"Caesar's," they replied.

¹⁷Then Jesus said to them, "Give back to Caesar what is Caesar's and to God what is God's."

And they were amazed at him.

---

a 17 Isaiah 56:7   *b 17* Jer. 7:11   *c 19* Some early manuscripts *came, Jesus* manuscripts include here words similar to Matt. 6:15.   *f 11* Psalm 118:22,23   *d 22,23* Some early manuscripts *"If you have faith in God," Jesus answered, ²³"truly*   *e 26* Some   *g 14* A special tax levied on subject peoples, not on Roman citizens

Marriage at the Resurrection

[18]Then the Sadducees, who say there is no resurrection, came to him with a question. [19]"Teacher," they said, "Moses wrote for us that if a man's brother dies and leaves a wife but no children, the man must marry the widow and raise up offspring for his brother. [20]Now there were seven brothers. The first one married and died without leaving any children. [21]The second one married the widow, but he also died, leaving no child. It was the same with the third. [22]In fact, none of the seven left any children. Last of all, the woman died too. [23]At the resurrection[a] whose wife will she be, since the seven were married to her?"

[24]Jesus replied, "Are you not in error because you do not know the Scriptures or the power of God? [25]When the dead rise, they will neither marry nor be given in marriage; they will be like the angels in heaven. [26]Now about the dead rising — have you not read in the Book of Moses, in the account of the burning bush, how God said to him, 'I am the God of Abraham, the God of Isaac, and the God of Jacob'[b]? [27]He is not the God of the dead, but of the living. You are badly mistaken!"

The Greatest Commandment

[28]One of the teachers of the law came and heard them debating. Noticing that Jesus had given them a good answer, he asked him, "Of all the commandments, which is the most important?"

[29]"The most important one," answered Jesus, "is this: 'Hear, O Israel: The Lord our God, the Lord is one.[c] [30]Love the Lord your God with all your heart and with all your soul and with all your mind and with all your strength.'[d] [31]The second is this: 'Love your neighbor as yourself.'[e] There is no commandment greater than these."

[32]"Well said, teacher," the man replied. "You are right in saying that God is one and there is no other but him. [33]To love him with all your heart, with all your understanding and with all your strength, and to love your neighbor as yourself is more important than all burnt offerings and sacrifices."

[34]When Jesus saw that he had answered wisely, he said to him, "You are not far from the kingdom of God." And from then on no one dared ask him any more questions.

Whose Son Is the Messiah?

[35]While Jesus was teaching in the temple courts, he asked, "Why do the teachers of the law say that the Messiah is the son of David? [36]David himself, speaking by the Holy Spirit, declared:

> "'The Lord said to my Lord:
>> "Sit at my right hand
> until I put your enemies
>> under your feet."'[f]

[37]David himself calls him 'Lord.' How then can he be his son?"

The large crowd listened to him with delight.

Warning Against the Teachers of the Law

[38]As he taught, Jesus said, "Watch out for the teachers of the law. They like to walk around in flowing robes and be greeted with respect in the marketplaces, [39]and have the most important seats in the synagogues and the places of honor at banquets. [40]They devour widows' houses and for a show make lengthy prayers. These men will be punished most severely."

The Widow's Offering

[41]Jesus sat down opposite the place where the offerings were put and watched the crowd putting their money into the temple treasury. Many rich people threw in large amounts. [42]But a poor widow came and put in two very small copper coins, worth only a few cents.

[43]Calling his disciples to him, Jesus said, "Truly I tell you, this poor widow has put more into the treasury than all the others. [44]They all gave out of their wealth; but she, out of her poverty, put in everything — all she had to live on."

The Destruction of the Temple and Signs of the End Times

13 As Jesus was leaving the temple, one of his disciples said to him, "Look, Teacher! What massive stones! What magnificent buildings!"

[2]"Do you see all these great buildings?" replied Jesus. "Not one stone here will be left on another; every one will be thrown down."

[3]As Jesus was sitting on the Mount of Olives opposite the temple, Peter, James, John and Andrew asked him privately, [4]"Tell us, when will these things happen? And what will be the sign that they are all about to be fulfilled?"

[5]Jesus said to them: "Watch out that no one deceives you. [6]Many will come in my name, claiming, 'I am he,' and will deceive many. [7]When you hear of wars and rumors of wars, do not be alarmed. Such things must happen, but the end is still to come. [8]Nation will rise against nation, and kingdom against kingdom. There will be earthquakes in various places, and famines. These are the beginning of birth pains.

[9]"You must be on your guard. You will be handed over to the local councils and flogged in the synagogues. On account of me you will stand before governors and kings as witnesses to them. [10]And the gospel must first be preached to all nations. [11]Whenever you are arrested and brought to trial, do not worry beforehand about what to say. Just say whatever is given you at the time, for it is not you speaking, but the Holy Spirit.

---

[a] 23 Some manuscripts *resurrection, when people rise from the dead,*   [b] 26 Exodus 3:6   [c] 29 Or *The Lord our God is one Lord*   [d] 30 Deut. 6:4,5   [e] 31 Lev. 19:18   [f] 36 Psalm 110:1

[12] "Brother will betray brother to death, and a father his child. Children will rebel against their parents and have them put to death. [13] Everyone will hate you because of me, but the one who stands firm to the end will be saved.

[14] "When you see 'the abomination that causes desolation'[a] standing where it[b] does not belong — let the reader understand — then let those who are in Judea flee to the mountains. [15] Let no one on the housetop go down or enter the house to take anything out. [16] Let no one in the field go back to get their cloak. [17] How dreadful it will be in those days for pregnant women and nursing mothers! [18] Pray that this will not take place in winter, [19] because those will be days of distress unequaled from the beginning, when God created the world, until now — and never to be equaled again.

[20] "If the Lord had not cut short those days, no one would survive. But for the sake of the elect, whom he has chosen, he has shortened them. [21] At that time if anyone says to you, 'Look, here is the Messiah!' or, 'Look, there he is!' do not believe it. [22] For false messiahs and false prophets will appear and perform signs and wonders to deceive, if possible, even the elect. [23] So be on your guard; I have told you everything ahead of time.

[24] "But in those days, following that distress,

"'the sun will be darkened,
  and the moon will not give its light;
[25] the stars will fall from the sky,
  and the heavenly bodies will be shaken.'[c]

[26] "At that time people will see the Son of Man coming in clouds with great power and glory. [27] And he will send his angels and gather his elect from the four winds, from the ends of the earth to the ends of the heavens.

[28] "Now learn this lesson from the fig tree: As soon as its twigs get tender and its leaves come out, you know that summer is near. [29] Even so, when you see these things happening, you know that it[b] is near, right at the door. [30] Truly I tell you, this generation will certainly not pass away until all these things have happened. [31] Heaven and earth will pass away, but my words will never pass away.

The Day and Hour Unknown

[32] "But about that day or hour no one knows, not even the angels in heaven, nor the Son, but only the Father. [33] Be on guard! Be alert[d]! You do not know when that time will come. [34] It's like a man going away: He leaves his house and puts his servants in charge, each with their assigned task, and tells the one at the door to keep watch.

[35] "Therefore keep watch because you do not know when the owner of the house will come back — whether in the evening, or at midnight, or when the rooster crows, or at dawn. [36] If he comes suddenly, do not let him find you sleeping. [37] What I say to you, I say to everyone: 'Watch!' "

Jesus Anointed at Bethany

14 Now the Passover and the Festival of Unleavened Bread were only two days away, and the chief priests and the teachers of the law were scheming to arrest Jesus secretly and kill him. [2] "But not during the festival," they said, "or the people may riot."

[3] While he was in Bethany, reclining at the table in the home of Simon the Leper, a woman came with an alabaster jar of very expensive perfume, made of pure nard. She broke the jar and poured the perfume on his head.

[4] Some of those present were saying indignantly to one another, "Why this waste of perfume? [5] It could have been sold for more than a year's wages[e] and the money given to the poor." And they rebuked her harshly.

[6] "Leave her alone," said Jesus. "Why are you bothering her? She has done a beautiful thing to me. [7] The poor you will always have with you,[f] and you can help them any time you want. But you will not always have me. [8] She did what she could. She poured perfume on my body beforehand to prepare for my burial. [9] Truly I tell you, wherever the gospel is preached throughout the world, what she has done will also be told, in memory of her."

[10] Then Judas Iscariot, one of the Twelve, went to the chief priests to betray Jesus to them. [11] They were delighted to hear this and promised to give him money. So he watched for an opportunity to hand him over.

The Last Supper

[12] On the first day of the Festival of Unleavened Bread, when it was customary to sacrifice the Passover lamb, Jesus' disciples asked him, "Where do you want us to go and make preparations for you to eat the Passover?"

[13] So he sent two of his disciples, telling them, "Go into the city, and a man carrying a jar of water will meet you. Follow him. [14] Say to the owner of the house he enters, 'The Teacher asks: Where is my guest room, where I may eat the Passover with my disciples?' [15] He will show you a large room upstairs, furnished and ready. Make preparations for us there."

[16] The disciples left, went into the city and found things just as Jesus had told them. So they prepared the Passover.

[17] When evening came, Jesus arrived with the Twelve. [18] While they were reclining at the table eating, he said, "Truly I tell you, one of you will betray me — one who is eating with me."

---

[a] 14 Daniel 9:27; 11:31; 12:11   [b] 14,29 Or he   [c] 25 Isaiah 13:10; 34:4   [d] 33 Some manuscripts *alert and pray*   [e] 5 Greek *than three hundred denarii*   [f] 7 See Deut. 15:11.

[19]They were saddened, and one by one they said to him, "Surely you don't mean me?"

[20]"It is one of the Twelve," he replied, "one who dips bread into the bowl with me. [21]The Son of Man will go just as it is written about him. But woe to that man who betrays the Son of Man! It would be better for him if he had not been born."

[22]While they were eating, Jesus took bread, and when he had given thanks, he broke it and gave it to his disciples, saying, "Take it; this is my body."

[23]Then he took a cup, and when he had given thanks, he gave it to them, and they all drank from it.

[24]"This is my blood of the[a] covenant, which is poured out for many," he said to them. [25]"Truly I tell you, I will not drink again from the fruit of the vine until that day when I drink it new in the kingdom of God."

[26]When they had sung a hymn, they went out to the Mount of Olives.

Jesus Predicts Peter's Denial

[27]"You will all fall away," Jesus told them, "for it is written:

" 'I will strike the shepherd,
    and the sheep will be scattered.'[b]

[28]But after I have risen, I will go ahead of you into Galilee."

[29]Peter declared, "Even if all fall away, I will not."

[30]"Truly I tell you," Jesus answered, "today — yes, tonight — before the rooster crows twice[c] you yourself will disown me three times."

[31]But Peter insisted emphatically, "Even if I have to die with you, I will never disown you." And all the others said the same.

Gethsemane

[32]They went to a place called Gethsemane, and Jesus said to his disciples, "Sit here while I pray." [33]He took Peter, James and John along with him, and he began to be deeply distressed and troubled. [34]"My soul is overwhelmed with sorrow to the point of death," he said to them. "Stay here and keep watch."

[35]Going a little farther, he fell to the ground and prayed that if possible the hour might pass from him. [36]"Abba,[d] Father," he said, "everything is possible for you. Take this cup from me. Yet not what I will, but what you will."

[37]Then he returned to his disciples and found them sleeping. "Simon," he said to Peter, "are you asleep? Couldn't you keep watch for one hour? [38]Watch and pray so that you will not fall into temptation. The spirit is willing, but the flesh is weak."

[39]Once more he went away and prayed the same thing. [40]When he came back, he again found them sleeping, because their eyes were heavy. They did not know what to say to him.

[41]Returning the third time, he said to them, "Are you still sleeping and resting? Enough! The hour has come. Look, the Son of Man is delivered into the hands of sinners. [42]Rise! Let us go! Here comes my betrayer!"

Jesus Arrested

[43]Just as he was speaking, Judas, one of the Twelve, appeared. With him was a crowd armed with swords and clubs, sent from the chief priests, the teachers of the law, and the elders.

[44]Now the betrayer had arranged a signal with them: "The one I kiss is the man; arrest him and lead him away under guard." [45]Going at once to Jesus, Judas said, "Rabbi!" and kissed him. [46]The men seized Jesus and arrested him. [47]Then one of those standing near drew his sword and struck the servant of the high priest, cutting off his ear.

[48]"Am I leading a rebellion," said Jesus, "that you have come out with swords and clubs to capture me? [49]Every day I was with you, teaching in the temple courts, and you did not arrest me. But the Scriptures must be fulfilled." [50]Then everyone deserted him and fled.

[51]A young man, wearing nothing but a linen garment, was following Jesus. When they seized him, [52]he fled naked, leaving his garment behind.

Jesus Before the Sanhedrin

[53]They took Jesus to the high priest, and all the chief priests, the elders and the teachers of the law came together. [54]Peter followed him at a distance, right into the courtyard of the high priest. There he sat with the guards and warmed himself at the fire.

[55]The chief priests and the whole Sanhedrin were looking for evidence against Jesus so that they could put him to death, but they did not find any. [56]Many testified falsely against him, but their statements did not agree.

[57]Then some stood up and gave this false testimony against him: [58]"We heard him say, 'I will destroy this temple made with human hands and in three days will build another, not made with hands.' " [59]Yet even then their testimony did not agree.

[60]Then the high priest stood up before them and asked Jesus, "Are you not going to answer? What is this testimony that these men are bringing against you?" [61]But Jesus remained silent and gave no answer.

Again the high priest asked him, "Are you the Messiah, the Son of the Blessed One?"

[62]"I am," said Jesus. "And you will see the Son of Man sitting at the right hand of the Mighty One and coming on the clouds of heaven."

[63]The high priest tore his clothes. "Why do we need any more witnesses?" he asked. [64]"You have heard the blasphemy. What do you think?"

---

[a] 24 Some manuscripts *the new*   [b] 27 Zech. 13:7   [c] 30 Some early manuscripts do not have *twice.*   [d] 36 Aramaic for *father*

They all condemned him as worthy of death. [65]Then some began to spit at him; they blindfolded him, struck him with their fists, and said, "Prophesy!" And the guards took him and beat him.

Peter Disowns Jesus

[66]While Peter was below in the courtyard, one of the servant girls of the high priest came by. [67]When she saw Peter warming himself, she looked closely at him.

"You also were with that Nazarene, Jesus," she said.

[68]But he denied it. "I don't know or understand what you're talking about," he said, and went out into the entryway.[a]

[69]When the servant girl saw him there, she said again to those standing around, "This fellow is one of them." [70]Again he denied it.

After a little while, those standing near said to Peter, "Surely you are one of them, for you are a Galilean."

[71]He began to call down curses, and he swore to them, "I don't know this man you're talking about."

[72]Immediately the rooster crowed the second time.[b] Then Peter remembered the word Jesus had spoken to him: "Before the rooster crows twice[c] you will disown me three times." And he broke down and wept.

Jesus Before Pilate

15 Very early in the morning, the chief priests, with the elders, the teachers of the law and the whole Sanhedrin, made their plans. So they bound Jesus, led him away and handed him over to Pilate.

[2]"Are you the king of the Jews?" asked Pilate.

"You have said so," Jesus replied.

[3]The chief priests accused him of many things. [4]So again Pilate asked him, "Aren't you going to answer? See how many things they are accusing you of."

[5]But Jesus still made no reply, and Pilate was amazed.

[6]Now it was the custom at the festival to release a prisoner whom the people requested. [7]A man called Barabbas was in prison with the insurrectionists who had committed murder in the uprising. [8]The crowd came up and asked Pilate to do for them what he usually did.

[9]"Do you want me to release to you the king of the Jews?" asked Pilate, [10]knowing it was out of self-interest that the chief priests had handed Jesus over to him. [11]But the chief priests stirred up the crowd to have Pilate release Barabbas instead.

[12]"What shall I do, then, with the one you call the king of the Jews?" Pilate asked them.

[13]"Crucify him!" they shouted.

[14]"Why? What crime has he committed?" asked Pilate.

But they shouted all the louder, "Crucify him!"

[15]Wanting to satisfy the crowd, Pilate released Barabbas to them. He had Jesus flogged, and handed him over to be crucified.

The Soldiers Mock Jesus

[16]The soldiers led Jesus away into the palace (that is, the Praetorium) and called together the whole company of soldiers. [17]They put a purple robe on him, then twisted together a crown of thorns and set it on him. [18]And they began to call out to him, "Hail, king of the Jews!" [19]Again and again they struck him on the head with a staff and spit on him. Falling on their knees, they paid homage to him. [20]And when they had mocked him, they took off the purple robe and put his own clothes on him. Then they led him out to crucify him.

The Crucifixion of Jesus

[21]A certain man from Cyrene, Simon, the father of Alexander and Rufus, was passing by on his way in from the country, and they forced him to carry the cross. [22]They brought Jesus to the place called Golgotha (which means "the place of the skull"). [23]Then they offered him wine mixed with myrrh, but he did not take it. [24]And they crucified him. Dividing up his clothes, they cast lots to see what each would get.

[25]It was nine in the morning when they crucified him. [26]The written notice of the charge against him read: THE KING OF THE JEWS.

[27]They crucified two rebels with him, one on his right and one on his left. [28][d] [29]Those who passed by hurled insults at him, shaking their heads and saying, "So! You who are going to destroy the temple and build it in three days, [30]come down from the cross and save yourself!" [31]In the same way the chief priests and the teachers of the law mocked him among themselves. "He saved others," they said, "but he can't save himself! [32]Let this Messiah, this king of Israel, come down now from the cross, that we may see and believe." Those crucified with him also heaped insults on him.

The Death of Jesus

[33]At noon, darkness came over the whole land until three in the afternoon. [34]And at three in the afternoon Jesus cried out in a loud voice, *"Eloi, Eloi, lema sabachthani?"* (which means "My God, my God, why have you forsaken me?").[e]

[35]When some of those standing near heard this, they said, "Listen, he's calling Elijah."

[36]Someone ran, filled a sponge with wine vinegar, put it on a staff, and offered it to Jesus to drink. "Now leave him alone. Let's see if Elijah comes to take him down," he said.

---

[a] 68 Some early manuscripts *entryway and the rooster crowed*   [b] 72 Some early manuscripts do not have *the second time*.   [c] 72 Some early manuscripts do not have *twice*.
[d] 28 Some manuscripts include here words similar to Luke 22:37.   [e] 34 Psalm 22:1

[37] With a loud cry, Jesus breathed his last.

[38] The curtain of the temple was torn in two from top to bottom. [39] And when the centurion, who stood there in front of Jesus, saw how he died,[a] he said, "Surely this man was the Son of God!"

[40] Some women were watching from a distance. Among them were Mary Magdalene, Mary the mother of James the younger and of Joseph,[b] and Salome. [41] In Galilee these women had followed him and cared for his needs. Many other women who had come up with him to Jerusalem were also there.

The Burial of Jesus

[42] It was Preparation Day (that is, the day before the Sabbath). So as evening approached, [43] Joseph of Arimathea, a prominent member of the Council, who was himself waiting for the kingdom of God, went boldly to Pilate and asked for Jesus' body. [44] Pilate was surprised to hear that he was already dead. Summoning the centurion, he asked him if Jesus had already died. [45] When he learned from the centurion that it was so, he gave the body to Joseph. [46] So Joseph bought some linen cloth, took down the body, wrapped it in the linen, and placed it in a tomb cut out of rock. Then he rolled a stone against the entrance of the tomb. [47] Mary Magdalene and Mary the mother of Joseph saw where he was laid.

Jesus Has Risen

16 When the Sabbath was over, Mary Magdalene, Mary the mother of James, and Salome bought spices so that they might go to anoint Jesus' body. [2] Very early on the first day of the week, just after sunrise, they were on their way to the tomb [3] and they asked each other, "Who will roll the stone away from the entrance of the tomb?"

[4] But when they looked up, they saw that the stone, which was very large, had been rolled away. [5] As they entered the tomb, they saw a young man dressed in a white robe sitting on the right side, and they were alarmed.

[6] "Don't be alarmed," he said. "You are looking for Jesus the Nazarene, who was crucified. He has risen! He is not here. See the place where they laid him. [7] But go, tell his disciples and Peter, 'He is going ahead of you into Galilee. There you will see him, just as he told you.'"

[8] Trembling and bewildered, the women went out and fled from the tomb. They said nothing to anyone, because they were afraid.[c]

[The earliest manuscripts and some other ancient witnesses do not have verses 9–20.]

[9] *When Jesus rose early on the first day of the week, he appeared first to Mary Magdalene, out of whom he had driven seven demons.* [10] *She went and told those who had been with him and who were mourning and weeping.* [11] *When they heard that Jesus was alive and that she had seen him, they did not believe it.*

[12] *Afterward Jesus appeared in a different form to two of them while they were walking in the country.* [13] *These returned and reported it to the rest; but they did not believe them either.*

[14] *Later Jesus appeared to the Eleven as they were eating; he rebuked them for their lack of faith and their stubborn refusal to believe those who had seen him after he had risen.*

[15] *He said to them, "Go into all the world and preach the gospel to all creation.* [16] *Whoever believes and is baptized will be saved, but whoever does not believe will be condemned.* [17] *And these signs will accompany those who believe: In my name they will drive out demons; they will speak in new tongues;* [18] *they will pick up snakes with their hands; and when they drink deadly poison, it will not hurt them at all; they will place their hands on sick people, and they will get well."*

[19] *After the Lord Jesus had spoken to them, he was taken up into heaven and he sat at the right hand of God.* [20] *Then the disciples went out and preached everywhere, and the Lord worked with them and confirmed his word by the signs that accompanied it.*

---

[a] 39 Some manuscripts *saw that he died with such a cry*   [b] 40 Greek *Joses*, a variant of *Joseph*; also in verse 47   [c] 8 Some manuscripts have the following ending between verses 8 and 9, and one manuscript has it after verse 8 (omitting verses 9-20): *Then they quickly reported all these instructions to those around Peter. After this, Jesus himself also sent out through them from east to west the sacred and imperishable proclamation of eternal salvation. Amen.*